IRELAND'S ISLANDS

IRELAND'S ISLANDS

LANDSCAPE, LIFE, AND LEGENDS

PETER SOMERVILLE-LARGE

WITH PHOTOGRAPHS BY DAVID LYONS

GILL & MACMILLAN

5142: IRELAND'S ISLANDS

Originally published by Quadrillion Publishing Limited 1999.

Published in Ireland by
Gill & Macmillan Ltd, Hume Avenue, Park West, Dublin 12
with associated companies throughout the world.
www.gillmacmillan.ie

copyright © Salamander Books Limited, 2000.

ISBN 0–7171–3207–2

Printed and bound in China

CONTENTS

N
W E
S

ATLANTIC OCEAN

Tory
Rathlin

DERRY

DONEGAL

BELFAST

Inishmurray

SLIGO

Achill

Clare

WESTPORT

Inishbofin

Lambay

DUBLIN
Ireland's Eye

GALWAY

IRELAND

The Aran Islands
Inishmore
Inishmaan
Inisheer

SHANNON AIRPORT

Scattery

LIMERICK

IRISH SEA

WEXFORD

WATERFORD

The Blasket Islands

TRALEE

Inishtooskert
Great Blasket
Inishvickillane

The Saltees

Beginish
Valentia

CORK

The Skelligs

Great Island

Dursey

0 10 20
km

Cape Clear
Sherkin

INTRODUCTION

I spent much of my boyhood on a small island in the Kenmare River in Co. Kerry. Around Illaunslea were other islands: Garinish with its lush trees and semi-tropical vegetation, owned by Lord Dunraven; windy and exposed Sherkey; the Pigeon Islands; and nearby Illaunagar. There is not a rock around Ireland that has not got a name. In the distance far out to sea were the Bull, the Cow and Calf rocks, and beyond, wrapped in mist, the cones of the Skelligs.

We indulged in the dreams of rich men—although my father's dream was not on the scale of Lord Dunraven, or other island owners like Lord Revelstoke or Harold Pinto, who spent fortunes on their creations at Lambay and Garinish. My experience on this holiday home had nothing in common with the lives of those who lived permanently in hardship on other islands, apart from a growing knowledge of the proximity of the sea in all its moods, the tides, and the sudden storms that could leave us marooned for a day or two.

No one has counted just how many islands there are around Ireland—one estimate has given one for every day of the year. Most are on the southwest and northwest coast and lie only a few miles off the mainland. Their shapes vary from the Skelligs, which have been called "the most dramatic structures in Western Europe," to the boomerang of cliffs that is Rathlin, and the dozens of small drumlin islands, flat as playing cards, that are scattered over Clew Bay. The limestone pavements of the Arans contrast with the tranquil fields of Inishbofin and the great headlands and cliffs of Tory and Achill. It is for the geologist to interpret these extraordinary variations that we see today: the volcanic stacks, glacial mouldings, sea caves, and the scouring effect of millions of years of Irish weather.

For thousands of years most islands that could offer something in the way of a living were inhabited. Each was home to a tribe that was really a small nation. There was a sense of nationhood, of absolute containment. Significantly, one or two, like Tory and Inishmurray, even elected their own kings. Isolation caused each community to differ from others in the way finches differ among the Galapagos Islands.

When an island becomes linked with the mainland, these differences are soon dissipated. Great Island has been merged into Co. Cork for many centuries. The individual nature of the people of Achill has dwindled since the bridge was constructed in 1888. It

has been said that Valentia's long history falls neatly into two parts: before the bridge and after it. In 1969, at about the same time Valentia was linked to Portmagee, a cable car was built between Dursey Island and the tip of the Beara peninsula, too late to keep the old community, which, with its current population of under ten, is on life support.

Today, observing people who are proud of their isolated community and its rich cultural inheritance and continue to struggle for its survival, we can unravel some of the mystery of why even the most inaccessible islands attracted inhabitants from prehistoric times. Those ancient settlers who have left behind kitchen middens, megalithic tombs, stone circles, cashels (usually, a fort with stone banks), promontory forts, and ancient field systems must have felt a similar sense of close identity. They had sailed over in the frailest of craft to create their lonely settlements. They found fertile soil, abundant fishing, and perhaps a sense of security, provided by the surrounding sea,

which prevailed until the arrival of the Vikings with their superior seamanship.

The seeking out of so many islands by early Christian hermits derived from the austerities of the Desert Fathers and the discipline of the

" *'a piece of land surrounded by water'*
strikes me as one of the most magical…
statements I have ever heard."

LAURENS VAN DER POST

Culdees. The physical discomforts were not much greater than those suffered by neolithic men and women. But the passion for lonely contemplation of the Divine Spirit manifest in the trackless wastes of the sea and the cry of sea birds was a celtic obsession that made this form of isolation a unique display of sanctity. For some time during the Dark Ages, Christianity depended on the prayers and meditations of St Enda on the Aran Islands, St

Ciaran on Cape Clear, St Molaise on Inishmurray, St Columcille restlessly flitting from island to island, and many more hermits who are unknown. Details of the lifestyle of these anchorite communities have been discovered through the excavations on Beginish and Church Island off Valentia. But the remains on Church Island are of the simplest dwelling places. Elsewhere monks combined holiness with architectural genius. It is hard to believe the saints performed greater miracles than those who supervised the erection of beehive huts on the summit of Skellig Michael or designed the maze on Inishmurray.

By the late Middle Ages, the Franciscan friars on Sherkin in West Cork were living in less extreme monastic surroundings. By then Vikings, pirates, clan chieftains looking for fishing dues, and formidable personalities like Grace O'Malley had played their part in island history. Later came the unpalatable fact that islands and their inhabitants became the spoils of conquest. At different times the

Arans were in the hands of the Digby and Guinness families, while Valentia belonged to the benevolent Knight of Kerry. In West Cork the Bechers owned both Sherkin and Cape Clear, while even the Skelligs, occupied by lighthouse keepers and sea birds, were in the hands of the Butlers. Only in 1907 were the Blaskets acquired from the Earl of Cork by the Congested Districts Board, while the last privately owned estate on Achill was taken from landlord control as recently as 1931. Even more recently, the Gage family on Rathlin continued the role of benevolent proprietor.

A defining moment came when the Congested Districts Board took over from the old landlords. Since the Board, established in 1891 to dispense assistance to poverty-stricken "congested districts," was an imperial creation during the period of British policy known as "Killing Home Rule with Kindness," its work in distributing land and giving grants for building houses, piers, and fishing has never been fully appreciated.

What else do these islands have in common besides their own individual enchantment? There is the odd watchtower perched on their highest point to look out for the French. They have a long history of shipwrecks. The lighthouses, some built and rebuilt with enormous difficulty, are still in the control of the body which in 1867 became the Commissioners of Irish Lights. It is hard not to feel some regret that the keepers, who for so long lived their separate and lonely lives apart from the islanders in these imposing buildings, have departed from all of them, and that computers have taken over.

For island people life was unremittingly hard. On the smaller islands there were no pubs or shops; supplies, including fuel, were carried over in frail boats. Not only were many communities cut off from the mainland by bad weather for weeks during the winter, but they had to endure a life without doctors or midwives. Those that got sick had to cure

ABOVE LEFT: Islands in Clew Bay, looking southwest from Rosturk toward Clare.

THIS PAGE: Two views of Great Skellig. The top picture shows the old lighthouse beyond the new one.

introduction 11

themselves with remedies like boiled milk and pepper, Beecham's pills, or seal oil. Without doctors people would die of undiagnosed illnesses like appendicitis.

The majority had to do without churches and priests. One of the most haunting images of Inishmurray is that of islanders meeting to say their own prayers at the exact time that a priest was holding Mass on the mainland. Religion was of the greatest importance for those who lived close to nature and to God.

There were the shortages that took place almost every winter, when people would be reduced to eating cockles, periwinkles, and even seaweed. There were the problems with livestock. How to tie down a struggling cow and manoeuvre it into a frail currach in order to take it over the waves to the mainland to be sold? When pigs were carried, their feet were muffled in sacks in case their trotters ripped the canvas. On islands near enough to the mainland, like those in Roaring Water Bay, animals would be swum across with a halter around their horns.

There was the constant lack of money. Fishing was a mainstay for most communities, but throughout the twentieth century fishing has been in decline. Although farming, lobstering, and the collection of gulls' eggs might provide seasonal income, there was little money for clothes or cigarettes or the penny to put on the plate when Mass on the mainland was attended. Mackerel and herring nets had to be bought, as had creosote and paint for the boats. English and American money became essential as sons and daughters who had emigrated sent a share of their earnings back to their families .

It was not all misery and deprivation. The joys of summer ranged from the hens beginning to lay, to the fish coming in, and the hay and potatoes growing. In winter there would be dancing to the fiddle and mouth organ, storytelling, and card games to the accompaniment of tea, poteen, and porter.

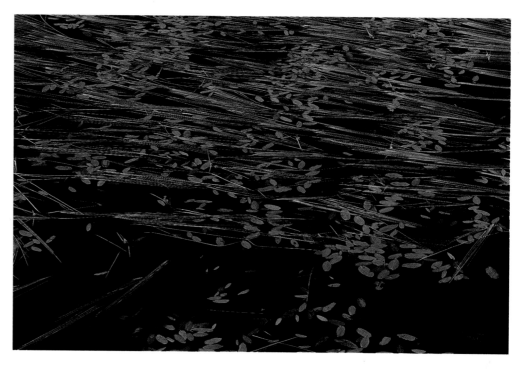

I interviewed a man who lived on an island in Roaring Water Bay who told me: "Living on an island makes a person apart. He has different values from the person on the mainland....The dependence of the island people on one another can never be appreciated by outsiders."

By the time the Irish Free State took over the role of the Congested Districts Board, the inhabitants of Irish-speaking islands like the Arans and the Blaskets had taken on a romantic image that brought them an extraordinary fame not only in Ireland, but abroad. They had a mythic appeal because they preserved a way of life that was seen to be unsullied by outside influences, in particular by the Anglo-Saxon tongue. Tory Island may have escaped this image of purity because it was too far offshore for a regular stream of visitors and scholars to visit and admire. Perhaps a literature might have been coaxed out of the Tory islanders in the same way as the men and women of the Blaskets were urged to create their marvellous books. Instead, on Tory it was painting that was encouraged by a discerning visitor.

The old ways that had survived on the islands but had vanished from the mainland—the use of the flail, fishing from currachs and coracles, booleying on Achill, and farming by the Rundale system on Tory—were sources of fascination for outsiders. On Aran, Robert Flaherty's film *Man of Aran* confirmed the romantic stereotype. In the years to come, islanders resented tourist interest in "aboriginal Irishness" and the things that were archaic and picturesque.

The writer Eibhlín Ní Shúileabháin heard an Aran islander who deplored "visitors going in and out of your house talking and talking and they on their own holidays and they at home having a comfortable home and no worrying during winter and summer would never believe the misfortunes on this island, no school, nor comfort, no road to success, no fishing—everything so dear and far away. Surely people could not live on air and sunshine." But visitors continued to admire the Arans as the last bastion of Gaelic culture. To

"The dependence of the island people on one another can never be appreciated by outsiders."

ROARING WATER BAY ISLANDER

Richard Hayward, writing about the islands in 1952, "there [was] something peculiarly intense and moving about the Aran scene, about the life of a primitive industrious community." "Primitive" was not a word to appeal to a proud people.

The long list of twentieth-century travellers captivated by island life includes artists like Augustus John, Seán Keating, and Paul Henry, and writers and personalities as diverse as Orson Welles and Brendan Behan. They all sought a world where traditional pastimes of singing, dancing, and storytelling survived, along with good conversation— described as "largely medieval, vigorous, direct, rich in oaths and assertions."

Popular tourism waited in the wings. Writing in 1936, the Dublin photographer Thomas Mason gave advice to any intending visitor. It was permissible to offer cigarettes to an islander, but never money; above all else the stranger must eschew any sense of superiority. Mason was addressing a select few. "I cannot visualise the type who enjoys Blackpool or the Isle of Man forsaking these resorts and vulgarising the Blaskets." One wonders what he would have thought of the boatloads of tourists who today descend on Irish islands during the summer months.

Meanwhile nothing could stop the decline in numbers. The failure of the fishing industry, the effects of isolation and monotony, and the consequences of wholesale emigration, have depleted island populations until today only a handful are still inhabited. Between 1956 and 1966, five islands off the Mayo coast were abandoned. Gola off the Donegal coast, Inishmurray off Sligo, and Scattery at the mouth of the Shannon were abandoned. In 1954 the 20 people remaining on the Great Blasket left their home and took up residence on the mainland.

Not everyone grieved. The young went first, eager to abandon their simple and beautiful lives and leave a dying world

inhabited by old people. And often the old, after a lifetime of hardship, departed without regret. A newspaper report of October 27, 1960, describing the exodus of the last six families and their assorted livestock from Inishark, the island beside Inishbofin, quoted "Thomas, 73, grandfather of baby Ann Lacey and father of the island" as saying: "I'll not be grieving for it. I've wanted to leave for years."

Today on many islands the decline in population has been stemmed to some extent as lifestyles change. The factors that have come to the aid of more distant islands include proper communication—a decent ferry service and a helicopter link with the mainland. Today islanders enjoy enhanced living conditions where most of the old drudgery has gone. Electricity and running water, backed by Gaeltacht grants and other subsidies, have helped to alleviate people's lives. (A Gaeltacht being an area where Irish is the everyday language of the majority of the people). There is now the ability to commute to and from the mainland. The Janus-headed amenity of television has become an essential during the long winters; card-playing, dancing, and other community activities have given way to watching soap operas and football games.

Where once you were lucky to find a bed, there are hotels, guesthouses, and hostels.

The 1996 study commissioned jointly by Bord Fáilte—the Irish Tourist Board—and An Taisce—the Irish National Trust—entitled *Tourism and the Landscape*, found that some communities fear being relegated to the status of "Indians on a reservation." The new words, "sustainable tourism," are being increasingly applied to Irish islands.

In the face of all the changes (and what some may consider degradation), much remains that is marvelous. There is the evidence of a rich and varied past, such as the magnificent complexes of Christian ruins on Inishmurray and Scattery. If people have gone, the birds flourish. Today many islands are officially recognised as wildlife sanctuaries. There are the ghosts. Landing on the deserted Blaskets, one hears the voice of Tomás Ó Criomhthainn: "I have written minutely of much that we did, for it was my wish that somewhere there should be a memorial of it all, and I have done my best to set it down—the character of the people about me—so that some record of it might live after us, for the likes of us will never be seen again."

The islands in this book are a fraction of the hundreds around the coast. Public perception of their importance has meant that they have been studied from a variety of viewpoints—archeological, social, and scientific. They are recognised as fragile areas of land that need our protection. No one can see the cloistered remains of Inishmurray or the deserted village on Achill without feeling profoundly moved. We enjoy the romantic feelings that islands provoke. Laurens van der Post has written: " 'a piece of land surrounded by water' strikes me as one of the most magical and eloquent of poetic statements I have ever heard." Our hearts long for the solitude and mystery of these places apart. "To reach felicity we must cross the water ... we must cross it to an island and a small one," wrote H. M. Tomlinson.

THE ARAN ISLANDS

Inishmore, Inishmaan, Inisheer

THE ARAN ISLANDS

PREVIOUS PAGE: The scattered village of Ballyhees is on Inisheer, the most easterly of the Aran Islands, easily accessible from Doolin in County Clare.

LEFT: The cargo ship *Plassey* was blown onto the limestone of Inisheer during a storm in 1960 and has been rusting away ever since.

ABOVE: Kilronan Harbour, at the south-eastern end of Inishmore, is the main destination of tourists. Here, until recently, hookers anchored, bringing their essential cargoes of turf, since the islands have no indigenous fuel.

Moulded by glacial activity during the Ice Age, the three Aran islands lie in a line across Galway Bay forming a barrier that runs roughly north-west/south-east. All three once belonged to a low limestone escarpment that has broken off in three uneven pieces (and a few fragments in the form of islets) from the Burren in Co. Clare. They are composed of bare carboniferous limestone pavements similar to those on the Burren.

The appearance of these pavements is of relentless stone, an impression intensified by the numerous erratics—huge granite boulders, brought over by an ice sheet from Connemara. Man has used the same common stone to create the patchwork of lacy walls, about one-and-a-half metres (five feet) high, the churches, beehive huts, dolmens, crosses, slabs, and stupendous cashels that have become as much a part of the landscape as the boulders. In addition, on Inishmore the unique wayside monuments, the *leachta cuimhne*, the "stones of memory," with their unusual English inscriptions, have been created from the ubiquitous limestone.

In Irish the islands are *Inis Oírr*, *Inis Meáin*, and *Árainn*. It is part of the changes that have taken place in the last 30 years that they are better known as Inisheer, Inishmaan, and Inishmore.

The plant life on the islands is similar to that of the Burren. In spring the gentians, bloody cranesbill, and mountain avens contrast brilliantly with the sullen grey of the stone; maidenhair fern grows in rock crevices. There are no trees, only low-growing shrubs like the spindle tree, hawthorn, and hazel. Only about one-third of the land area has been cultivated over the centuries as the islanders painstakingly created fields by piling layers of sand and seaweed on top of crushed rock.

Seaweed, known as the black weed, was used as fertiliser. Liam O'Flaherty, one of Inishmore's most famous sons, described in a short story, *Poor People*, the dismal labour of shivering seaweed gatherers in their squelching pampooties (rawhide shoes) gathering the weed, "slime covered, dribbling in with every wave." In the early twentieth century, up to seven hundred and fifty tons of kelp was exported annually. It took 20 tons of seaweed—of which there are 30 varieties—to make a ton of kelp. The little industry required much toil—the cutting and harvesting of weed, then the firing of the kilns in late June, sending up spirals of smoke into the sky.

The land holdings are traditionally very small, averaging about 6½ hectares (16 acres) to each householder, much of which is rock. Added to the difficulties of preparing and maintaining the little fields was the transportation of cattle to and from the mainland. Another permanent problem on Aran is the total lack of fuel; until recently hookers (small sailing boats) brought over turf from the mainland. Today, yellow propane gas canisters offer a more convenient means of doing the cooking and providing heating.

Until the American market collapsed in the 1930s, the autumn catch of mackerel was salted in barrels and sent to the United States. Robert Flaherty's *Man of Aran*, with its proud people silhouetted against the storms (still known on the island as "the film"), made the most of the spectacular difficulties of fishing—dropping a long line from the top of the cliffs of Inishmore for pollock, or chasing the basking shark for lamp oil, a form of hunting that had ceased long before Flaherty ever landed on Kilronan pier. "The exaggeration-est film ever made" has become part of the Aran legend and is shown most days at Kilronan. But some things were not exaggerated: the fishing, based on currachs and small hookers, that supported life up to a few decades ago, was always a perilous pursuit.

Currachs are made of a light framework of laths covered with tarred black canvas. In

TOP: Dún Eoghanachta ring fort on Inishmore, which has a terraced rampart and three house sites.
ABOVE: Waiting for passengers, Kilronan. Bicycles and minibuses offer tourists alternative transport.

their heyday, a crew, usually consisting of three men, rowed them with oars that were almost bladeless. They could carry a cargo of a tethered cow, a ton of potatoes, and up to twelve people. But whatever the skills of the boatmen, danger was always present. "The sea," wrote Thomas Mason, the photographer and author of *The Islands of Ireland*, published in 1936, "is both a blessing and a curse; a blessing because it enables the islanders to live, and a curse, because it is the cause of many tragedies. It robs the women of their men, and hardly a family on the islands has not lost a relative by drowning or exposure."

In an unpromising environment the Aran Islands have supported human habitation since the time of the legendary Celtic Firbolgs, who were reputed to have settled on Aran and Rathlin after their defeat by the Tuatha de Danaan. Later, Christian monks and hermits built their enchanting churches on the stony limestone wastes, and the Arans became known as "the Islands of Saints." St Enda's monastery was one of the earliest and at one time ranked supreme in Ireland. In the fifth century Enda, a Meath man, is reputed to have sailed to the Aran Islands on a stone. He made the islands his base and founded his monastery on Inishmore, from where he was largely responsible for the development of monasticism in Ireland on a systematised basis. His monastery was raided by Vikings in 1081, and its last recorded abbot died around 1400. St Columcille is also closely associated with the islands, and in due course his cult superseded that of St Enda.

> *"The sea is both a blessing and a curse...it enables the islanders to live and robs the women of their men"*
>
> THOMAS MASON

In medieval times the O'Flahertys and O'Briens contested the islands; later settlers included an English garrison. By 1841 the population of the three islands had reached 3500, but at the end of the century a pattern of departure had settled in, and a total of 1386 people lived there, according to the census of 1896. By then the islands had passed into the possession of a series of landlords and their agents, ranging from the Earl of Aran in 1662 to the Digby family and even the Guinness dynasty. It was only in 1921 that the Congested Districts Board returned the land to the people of Aran.

By then the islanders had become used to files of visitors, amazed and beguiled by the strange allure of the landscape, the spectacular antiquities, and the presence of grave, handsome, Irish-speaking people whose courtesy was noticeable and whose clothes were picturesque. The Arans became a symbol. The importance of the islands in myth and reality cannot be overstated—the three small islands were recognised as bastions of Gaelic culture. Infatuated visitors included savants and celebrities like John O'Donovan, William Wilde, Douglas Hyde, William Butler Yeats, and Lady Gregory, and artists like Augustus John, Jack Yeats, and Sean Keating. John Synge's name is forever linked to Aran.

In 1857 George Petrie visited Aran together with 70 "ethnologists and antiquarians" organised by Oscar Wilde's father, Sir William Wilde. They travelled over in the Trinity College yacht. Petrie's aim, together with his friend Eugene O'Curry, was to collect music. "On approaching a house, always lighted up by a blazing turf fire, it was surrounded by islanders, while the interior was crowded with figures....The minstrel—sometimes an old woman, sometimes a beau-

ABOVE LEFT: Dún Aonghasá, Inishmore. Defences include stone stakes known as chevaux-de-frise.
ABOVE RIGHT: The long stone wall of the promontory fort of Dún Ducathair cuts it off from the sea.

tiful girl or a young man—was seated on a low stool in a chimney corner....The song having been given, O'Curry wrote down the Irish words, when Petrie's work began. The singer recommended, stopping at a signal from him at every two or three bars of the melody to permit the writing of notes... twenty-eight airs were harvested on Aranmore from the seventh to the nineteenth of September."

Later enthusiasts included the teenage Orson Welles, who in 1930 admired the "fine Erin men in indigo and homespun and beautiful (I use the word unhesitatingly) and smiling colleens in nice red skirts and sienna jackets." When the writer Kevin Crossley-Holland came to Inishmore in the 1970s, when women "of haunting beauty" still wore red petticoats, he was overwhelmed. "It's so lovely," he exclaimed, to be told: "Only a visitor like yourself would find it lovely."

A more recent newcomer who has observed and interpreted the islands is Tim Robinson, whose *Stones of Aran* brings a new insight not only into the physical landscape and man's background on the islands stretching back for more than four thousand years, but also to the new dangers imposed by "the material destructiveness of modern life which all too rapidly impinges on Aran."

With the Atlantic keeping them apart, the three islands are very different. Kevin Crossley-Holland was told that "no girl at all on Árainn would marry to Inishmaan or Inisheer—it would be too isolated there." Although this is no longer the case, with easy access by sea and air—there are year-round daily flights to all three islands—each island maintains its individuality.

Inishmore, or Árainn, by far the largest of the three, is 12 kilometres (eight miles) long and three kilometres (two miles) wide and consists of 3090 hectares (7635 acres). The chief port is Kilronan, to which a hovercraft will bring you rapidly from the Galway shore.

The first target for most tourists, accessible by minibus, is the great stone fort of Dún Aonghasa, perilously poised in concentric half circles of stone walls on a cliff 90 metres (300 feet) above the sea. In the height of summer the stream of visitors walking up to Dún Aonghasa resembles pictures of the Klondike during the gold rush.

Away from the crowd it is better to walk near another stretch of cliff where the waves send up masses of spray and foam, or along the boreens and across the limestone to search out Inishmore's ancient heritage. Other forts that have blended with the surrounding stone for thousands of years are Dún Ducathair, the "Black Fort," a promontory fort almost as spectacular as Dún Aonghasa, and Dún Eoghanachta, the inland cashel with two walls on the highest land on Inishmore. Teampall Benen, perched on a limestone ridge with high-pitched gables reaching to the sky, is a fifth-century oratory dedicated to St Benen, St Patrick's successor to the See of Armagh. There are two round towers: St Eany's, of which only fragments remain, and Turmartin, at the island's eastern end in the townland of Killeany. Turmartin is thought to be St Gregory's grave, and sailors dip their sails as they pass it. East of Killeany is Tighlagheany, the household of St Enda,

reputed to be the holiest place on Aran, where 120 saints are buried. In Kilmurvey townland *Teampall Brecan*—St Brecan's Church—has in its graveyard St Brecan's grave and a stone with the inscription "VII ROMANI"—seven Roman saints.

But on a summer's day, who cares whether John Rawson built Arkin's Castle in 1587 or whether the enchanting *Teampall an Cheathair Alainn* translates as the Church of the Four Beautiful Saints? (The names of these handsome holy men, who are buried nearby, are St Fursey, St Brendan, St Conall

and St Berchall). It may be more pleasant to relax on one of the headlands looking out to sea, as Synge did on Inishmaan: "there is no wind, and no definite light. Aranmore seems to sleep upon a mirror, and the hills of Connemara look so near that I am troubled by the width of the Bay that lies before them, touched this morning with individual expression one sees sometime in a lake…."

Inisheer, the smallest island and nearest to Doolin on the Clare coast, has also succumbed to the demands of tourism, but unlike Inishmore, its small size—566 hectares (1400 acres)—makes it less easy to lose oneself in the past. Ancient churches are there: *Cill Ghobnait*—Gobnet's Church—with its round-headed east window, and the Grave of the Seven Daughters surrounded by a stone enclosure. O'Brien's Castle above the harbour, thought to date from the fourteenth century, is built within the walls of a celtic fort a thousand years older. Limestone pavement spreads beside the eastern shore, and the sand has its hold. The half-buried chapel of *Teampall Chaomháin,* the church of St Cavan, is cleared of sand on the saint's feast day. Irish is spoken freely as on other islands. But the youth hostel and the cheery pub full of tourists are symptoms of a loss of the old tradition, and the crowds of young people who spill over from Doolin are more interested in the *craic* than in the past.

Of the three islands, Inishmaan, in the middle, which consists of 910 hectares (2252 acres), has best kept its culture. There is a strong cooperative spirit at work here to preserve the language and something of the old lifestyle, and fishing and farming are still

ABOVE LEFT: Teampall Chaomháin, half-buried in sand, which is cleared on the saint's feast day, June 14th.
BELOW LEFT: O'Brien's Castle, a ruined fourteenth-century tower, stands above the houses of Inisheer in a ring fort which is a thousand years older.
ABOVE: This altar slab is within the ruin of Teampall Chaomháin.

carried out to a greater extent than elsewhere. Children playing and young men belonging to the football team do their talking and shouting and exchange of jokes in Irish. The talk in the pub is the sound that Kevin Crossley-Holland recalled in the early '70s on Inishmore—"a sustained susurrus like the hum of bees—or the sound of a distant summer sea." The island is recognised as the least

the hookers that brought the precious fuel from Connemara, the pride of owning a currach still remains. In spring the black craft are being got ready for the sea. The most eagerly fought contests on the island are the currach races in August.

"Can you hear the waves?" an old islander asked when I met him that day. "When you hear them that's a sign of good weather."

atmosphere he recorded. "The walls have been toned by the turf-smoke to a soft brown that blends with the grey earth-colour of the floor. Many sorts of fishing tackle and the nets and oilskins of the men, are hung upon the walls or among the open rafters; and right overhead, under the thatch, there is a whole cow skin from which they make pampooties."

Dún Conor looms above the MacDonagh

spoilt Gaeltacht area in the country. Here there are virtually no bungalows, no pony traps lying in wait for hire, and the soft common tongue is Irish.

On the warm, windless spring day when I arrived, a cuckoo's call broke the silence. The old landscape is undefiled, small stony fields are studded with flowers of limestone. Other fields enclosed by stone are laid out with lines of vegetables, the huge beaches are empty, and the blush of hawthorn grows among the terraces. If the old welcoming scent of burning turf has become a thing of the past, like

Padraic Pearse came to Inishmaan to learn the language, and in 1898 John Synge, who had studied Gaelic in Trinity, arrived by currach, having spent two weeks at the modest Atlantic Hotel in Kilronan. In the small straddling village, he stayed in the little cottage belonging to the MacDonagh family, near the church and the post office. He would come here each summer until 1902 and gain the material for his plays, helped by "the drone of Gaelic voices coming from the kitchen."

There are plans to restore the little ruin, though it would be hard to re-create the

cottage. "One of the largest Dúns or pagan forts, on the islands, is within a stone's throw of my cottage, and I often stroll up there after a dinner of eggs or salt pork to smoke drowsily on the stones."

ABOVE LEFT: With an absence of gates, the shoulder-high dry-stone walls must be breached to enter a field and the stones replaced.
ABOVE RIGHT: Looking across the sands of Trawmore on Inishmore toward the west shore of Inishmaan.
OPPOSITE: In the distance, the Cliffs of Moher on the Clare coast, seen from the eastern tip of Inisheer.

Not far off, the modern church, dedicated in 1939, has an altar by James Pearse, the father of Padraic Pearse, and dazzling windows by Harry Clarke's studio. A group of old women coming out after Mass still wear traditional shawls and red skirts. "The red dresses of the women," wrote Synge, "…give a glow of almost Eastern richness." But the men's thick trousers of homespun tweed held up by criosanna, their flannel shirts dyed indigo, with stand-up collars and leg-of-mutton sleeves, worn with wide-awake hats and

"Aran…seems to me one of the most enchanting and interesting spots in Europe…"

HUBERT BUTLER

rawhide slippers or pampooties (a word of Javanese origin) are memories, only recorded in the work of painters like Sean Keating, Jack Yeats, and Augustus John.

In the '50s Hubert Butler could write: "I am tempted to use the language of hyperbole about Aran. It seems to me one of the most

enchanting and interesting spots in Europe, since it has held to a precious beauty and simplicity which the rest of Europe is disastrously discarding." Since that time, inevitably, much of the grandeur associated with the men and women of Aran, cultivated by isolation and hardship, has eroded. But in spite of strident changes, it is not yet extinct, and on Inishmaan there is a sustained effort to maintain the best features of the old Gaelic society. The landscape endures, the weird beauty of stone.

INISHBOFIN

INISHBOFIN

PREVIOUS PAGE: Ship
Sound divides Trá Ghael,
the southwestern strand
at Westquarter, from
the deserted island
of Inishark.
LEFT: Hookers,
once essential fishing
vessels, now take part
in the annual Kinvara
Regatta.
ABOVE: Looking east
over the site of St
Colman's monastery
toward the island of
Inishlyon.

Inishbofin, which has an area of 970 hectares (3¾ square miles), lies 12 kilometres (eight miles) off the Galway coast. From Cleggan the ferry makes a quick crossing, carrying tourists armed with video cameras. If they look behind, they have the towering background of the Twelve Pins and the mountains behind Clew Bay, dominated by the cone of Croagh Patrick. In this sea area are numerous other islands. Some are uninhabited islets like Davillaun, Inishskinny, Inishlyon, Low Island, and High Island, where once a woman cutting seaweed was marooned and gave birth to a child—until she was rescued she was fed miraculously for a week. To the west, separated by the narrow Ships' Sound, is Inishark, which had its own community until about thirty years ago.

In an ecclesiastical record dating back to the seventh century, Inishbofin is referred to as *Insula Vitulae Albae*, "the Island of the White Cow." The name derives from a Gaelic folk tale of which there are several versions. The island was enchanted, hidden in a mist, until two fishermen landed by chance on its shores and lit a fire by a lake, breaking the spell. They saw an old woman driving a white cow along the strand; when she struck her, the animal turned into a rock. The fishermen in their turn struck the witch, and they, too, became rocks.

Enchanted or not, people have lived on Bofin for thousands of years. Kitchen middens have been found, neolithic field systems, hut sites, *fulachta fia*—cooking sites—dating to the Bronze Age, and promontory forts belonging to Iron Age man, who lived here around 500B.C. The motivation of early saints and hermits is understandable. However, why should early man have been attracted to such a lonely outpost when the mainland was a short distance away, even in the most primitive of currachs? Between the men who discarded the shells that made the middens and St Colman and his monks, who came here in the seventh century, there is an unexplained gap of 6000 years.

The remains of a fourteenth-century church marks the spot where St Colman founded his monastery in the sixth century. Colman was preceded by other holy men—St Fechin, for example—who are remembered by their holy wells. Perhaps the presence of these saints and their good deeds has cancelled out the bloodshed associated with later episodes in the island's history. Among them was the destruction of St Colman's monastery by Sir John D'Arcy in 1334.

The harbour and pier are approached by a deep inlet just over a kilometre (three-quarters of a mile) long, guarded by rocks. They include the Bishop's Rock, where the English are said to have chained an unfortunate Bishop of Clonfert, leaving him to drown on the incoming tide. But there is no historical evidence of this, and a similar lurid story is told of the Christian chieftain Guairin, who came to a similar end on Inishbofin.

To the right of the inlet at the sea end is a confused ruin known as Bosco's Castle, a jumble of grey stone walls suspended above a cliff. Its earliest mention in history is as a fort held by Don Bosco, a Spanish pirate, who put a chain across the harbour and threw into the sea anyone who landed without his permission—a variation of walking the plank. There was a connection between Don Bosco and the O'Malleys with whom the pirate had an

alliance. Grace O'Malley occupied his castle from time to time, using the harbour for her ships and impounding the sailing craft of vanquished islanders during her stay here. The chain across the harbour may have been hers.

After she died, Inishbofin became the property of the Bourke clan, but was repossessed by the O'Malleys in 1641. In the subsequent Cromwellian wars, Inishbofin was one of the last places in Ireland to surrender to the English, in February 1653. Subsequently the buildings of Bosco's Castle were converted into a typical star-shaped fort of the seventeenth century and were used as a garrison by Cromwell's soldiers, who captured the island in 1652; later it became a prison for priests awaiting transportation to the West Indies.

So much history for such a small island was the result of two factors—the fine, natural, deep-water harbour, and the fishing. The stretch of water known as Bofin Bank was regarded as one of the richest fishing areas on the entire Irish coast, attracting fishermen from the continent of Europe. Local clans looked for fees from visiting fishermen, and the squabbles between the O'Malleys and

O'Flahertys over control of the fishing grounds were fuelled by fishing dues.

In the nineteenth century Bofin was famous for herring caught in nets, and cod and ling taken on the long line. Herring was primarily a winter catch, while mackerel was taken during the summer. Fleets of hookers from the Claddagh in Galway, Westport, and elsewhere would sail to Bofin Bank, although a figure of 10,000 fishermen assembling in these waters during a fishery may be exaggerated.

ABOVE LEFT: Bosco's Castle dominates the entrance to Bofin harbour at Barracks Point.
BELOW LEFT: The West's own paper, *The Western People*, of Saturday, November 6, 1948.
BELOW: A swell between Inishbofin and the Connemara coast.

Although the islanders themselves depended on fishing, their small craft were no match for the fleets from outside. However, fishing, augmented by subsistence farming, and probably a little poteen-distilling, continued to support a substantial population. In 1873, the Bofin fleet had 52 boats: nobbies, púcáns, rowboats, and currachs.

By then the island had long been in the hands of landlords and their agents. Some seem to have conformed to the traditional ogre image, like Lord Sligo's agent, Henry Hildebrand, remembered as "a selfish tyrannical brute" who encouraged "soupers" or proselytising missionaries to preach on the island. In 1876 Thomas Allies acquired Bofin and Shark from Henry Wilberforce, in payment of a debt. The Catholic Allies family broke the normal pattern by being well liked.

In 1907 the Land Commission took possession of the island from the last landlord, Cyril Allies, and through the Congested Districts Board transferred ownership of holdings to the islanders. The Board built stone houses to replace mud-walled thatched cottages, gave grants for boats, and built a new pier and a curing house for fish.

Because of outside economics, fishing as a way of life was already on the decline by 1927, the year of the Cleggan disaster. In those days fishing took place at night in open boats, each with a crew of four or six men. On the night of the disaster, when a combination of frost, rain, and a terrible wind brought catastrophe, fishermen were reluctant to discard their precious nets and hung onto them until it was too late. One fisherman's body was found enmeshed in a net. It is painful to read the

accounts of survivors, temporarily blinded by sea spray, rowing for 12 hours and listening to screams in the darkness from neighbouring boats as the waves overturned them. In all, 28 men were drowned, nine of them from Bofin. In his poem on the disaster Richard Murphy wrote how:

In a common grave that was dug in the
*   sand-dunes ...*
They laid side by side the deal-board coffins,
Lowering them on ropes, then shovelled the
*   fine sand*
Which whisperingly slid round their recent
*   companions ...*

The tragedy, which took the heart out of the fishing community, marked the end of drift-net fishing. The wage earners had either drowned or were too fearful to go to sea again in their heavy rowboats. Just outside St Colman's Church, overlooking the pier and harbour, a simple cross by the sculptor John Behan commemorates the known islanders of Inishark and Inishbofin who have lost their lives at sea; the names of the nine from Bofin who died that stormy October night are recorded.

For a period up to the Emergency in 1939, lobstering from currachs took over, largely to

supply the French market. Today, in spite of over-fishing, a certain amount of lobster fishing continues. But today few fishing boats remain, and the little port of West Town is generally quiet.

There is a complete absence of spoken Irish on Bofin. Where Aran and the Blaskets retained a living tradition of Gaelic, on Bofin the language was no more than a memory by the end of the nineteenth century. Various reasons have been put forward, such as the

yoke of landlordism, the prospect of emigration where Irish would be useless, and the forced application of English in schools. During the nineteenth century a little stick called a *cloigeann capaill*, or tally, was hung on a string around a child's neck, and if he or she spoke Irish, a notch was put on the stick. When the notches reached a certain number, the child would be beaten.

The early demise of Irish meant that Inishbofin never benefited from Gaeltacht grants after the new state was founded. The Irish names survive as landmarks, and each small field, each rock, cliff, and headland is remembered—*Loch Bó Finne*—the Enchanted Lake of the White Cow; *Leim Laitico*—The Fool's Jump; *Carraig Sheamais*—Seamas' Rock; *Gap na Siog*— The Fairy Gap; and *Bóithrín na gCapall*—the Little Road of the Horses at Westquarter Hill, where horses were driven carrying turf from the bog.

Although two hotels and a hostel cater for visitors, and various boozy festivals are held in the summer months, the island still has peace and beauty. Some tourists sip their drinks at Day's Hotel, once the seat of the Allies family. They take their ease on an island described by the *Shell Guide* as "a pleasant place for a simple holiday."

This is an island easy to explore and love, walking the High and Low roads past reedy lakes and cliffs. At the small East Village a line of fishermen's houses—many done up as holiday homes—faces a huge sandy beach and the ruin of the Board's curing sheds. Inland, there are traditional haycocks, and hens scuttle outside farmhouse doors.

Inishbofin appears to have turned the economic corner and enjoys a measure of prosperity, unlike its neighbour Inishark, whose own saint, St Leo, did not intervene to save the smaller island from losing its people. A footnote of history was the stark account by a journalist of the final exodus from Shark in October 1966: "I have watched the last survivors…of six families moving out like a garrison surrendering after a lifetime's siege. Their livestock included thirteen cows, twelve dogs, ten donkeys, eight cats, scores of hens, a hundred sheep and a stack of hay." From Bofin you can look out on the empty houses and fields to the church on Shark where St Leo's sacred bell was kept.

There is hope that those who continue to live on the treasure that is Inishbofin, with its lakes and cliffs, its small green fields and holy places, will escape Shark's fate. And the birds will flourish. Here is one place in Ireland where the corncrake survives, thanks to ancient farming practices and a grant to farmers not to cut their hay until August. The raucous croak proclaiming territory is still to be heard in the fields at the island's east end. May the future for the corncrake and the 177 people who live on Bofin today be bright!

CENTRE TOP: A session in Days Bar. Islandman Des O'Halloran is an accomplished fiddler.

BELOW, FAR LEFT: Traditional hayfields, on the south shore, contribute to the gentle beauty of the Inishbofin landscape.

BELOW, LEFT: The pad for the helicopter, for emergencies, links islanders to the mainland.

RIGHT: The western cliffs at Dún Mór.

CLARE

CLARE

Clare Island measures eight kilometres (five miles) long by five kilometres (three miles) across. Green and fertile, it stands like a sentinel guarding Clew Bay, five-and-a-half kilometres (three-and-a-half miles) from the nearest mainland point at Roonagh Pier, Co. Mayo. Beyond the scattering of little flat islets that fill the bay, the commanding crown of Knockmore on Clare, which rises to 457 metres (1500 feet) above sea level, gives the island an appearance that has been described as "sphinxlike."

Clare's extraordinarily varied landscape, which has been compared to "an Ireland in miniature," led it to be chosen more than eighty years ago for one of the most comprehensive natural history surveys ever given to an island around the British Isles. Under the direction of the botanist Robert Lloyd Praeger, over a hundred field workers collected material from 1909 to 1911, which were published by the Royal Irish Academy in a series of 67 reports.

From that time until today, the unique geology and the many different types of rocks concentrated here, which date back a possible thousand million years, have continued to attract scientific attention. The oldest fossil found in Ireland (of a sponge more than five

PREVIOUS PAGE: These jagged cliffs are off the southwest coast, below Knockmore.
LEFT: Until very recently, the flocks of sheep denuded island pasture to a dangerous extent.
ABOVE RIGHT: Wayside plants—montbretia, purple loosestrife, nettles, and horsetails.

million years old) was discovered in beds of chert in the townland of Ballytoughey More. There is sandstone, and limestone supporting a saxifrage flora, while molten rocks and hot gases arising from a curious geological feature known as the "Leic Fault" have provided barite, graphite, and silica, indicating that gold could be here, as it is on Croagh Patrick across the bay. Plant spores found on other rocks are evidence of their links with eastern Canada. Stumps of ancient trees are traces of old forests that vanished soon after man arrived with his ruthless slash-and-burn techniques. There have been no trees for centuries; islanders have used fuel from the bogs.

For many years the richness of Clare's archeological heritage was neglected. Until the 1970s, history only went back to medieval times. "Nothing is known about the early history of the island," stated Peter Harbison's *Guide to National and Historical Monuments of Ireland*, first published in 1970. It was not until 1989 that this statement could be turned on its head, during the first Clare Island Symposium, when the archeologist Paul Gosling of Galway University was responsible for the discovery of a number of *fulachta fia*—cooking sites—and a court tomb. Immediately, the history of Clare Island had

been put back by over five thousand years.

Since then, other discoveries have indicated the presence of early man: a court tomb, inscribed and decorated stones, promontory forts like that of Doonagul, the remains of a cashel and beehive huts, and traces of an Iron Age field system. It seems astonishing that so much could have been unknown for so long; the reason generally put forward is that in spite of the Clare survey, which drew the attention of many scientists, the island, being English-speaking, offered none of the glowing attractions of Aran and was consequently ignored by archeologists.

Among the ancient sites noted before the great discoveries of the 1990s are two holy wells. *Tober Feile Mhuire*, the Well of Mary's Feast, is situated to the north of Clare Abbey, on what may have been an earlier druidic site. The abbey, built by Cistercian monks, is a little building whose interior roof was once covered with paintings. Vivid traces remain of animals which recall decorative motifs in the Book of Kells: dragons, monsters spitting fire, birds, rabbits, and a harper.

Other more recent dominant buildings are the forlorn signal tower, the lighthouse that

Clare's extraordinarily varied landscape...
has been compared to "an Ireland in miniature"

overlooks the northern edge of cliffs and, of course, Grace O'Malley's castle. The scene that greets the boat on arriving at an island is often the picture that remains longest in the traveller's mind. Just outside the harbour beside the small settlement of houses and the hotel stands the castle, one of 11 that the O'Malleys once controlled. A grey stone shell that has no battlements, during the nineteenth century it was converted for the use of coastguards. But it has a proud history. While it is thought that Grace O'Malley did not build this castle, which had previously been used more as a summer residence, it became her base and stronghold. The three-storey tower, standing on a rocky headland overlooking the sea, enabled her to keep an eye on enemy and friend. No other Irish island can boast such a dominant figure; long before Women's Lib, thrice-married Grace imposed her will, amassed wealth and enlarged her influence with her fleet of galleys, practising piracy, policing foreign ships travelling past her island, and collecting fishing tolls.

Her father was Owen *Dubhdara* (Black Oak) O'Malley, the chief of the clan. At the same time that she was struggling against the inroads of English power, one of the great ships of the Armada, the 1160-ton galley *El Gran Grin*, struck the southwestern tip of the island. All the 100 survivors were put to the sword by Grace's father, a fate that many other Armada sailors met along the west coast of Ireland.

Although the family motto was "Invincible on Land and Sea," by the middle of the sixteenth century the advance of Elizabethan

ABOVE: Ridge and furrow cultivation near Kill. The hills of South Mayo are visible in the distance.

military forces, headed in Mayo by Sir Richard Bingham, slowly overwhelmed the O'Malley territories. At one time Grace was fighting the English, at another submitting to them. She had a spell of prison in Dublin. She impressed Sir Henry Sidney when he met her in Galway in 1576. "There came to me a most famous feminine sea-captain called Grany Imallye and offered her services unto me wheresoever I would command her, with 3 galleys and 200 fighting men, either in Ireland or Scotland. She brought with her her husband, for she was as well by sea as by land more than Mrs Mate with him."

At the age of 63 Grace O'Malley met the English Queen Elizabeth, sailing in one of her galleys around Ireland and up the Thames to Greenwich. She is said to have arrived barefoot, and Elizabeth was obliged to raise her hand high as the Irish woman was taller.

CENTRE TOP: A detail of the arms of the O'Malleys on the altar tomb in Clare Abbey.

BELOW LEFT: For many years the island economy has been dependent on sheep.

BELOW RIGHT: Weaving and other small-scale industries provide an alternative to farming.

Their conversation in a mutual language, Latin, recorded in the State Papers, resulted in the release of her imprisoned son and her submission to the Crown.

Grace's burial place is thought to be in the canopied tomb in Clare Abbey, a short distance up the road from the harbour. There is a strong tradition that her skull was on display decked with ribbons and two gold earrings; Thomas Mason was shown a skull unornamented in a recess in a wall, which he was told was hers.

Clare supported a large population for centuries. Crops on its fertile soil produced corn, which paid the rent, and potatoes for consumption. By the early nineteenth century 1600 people lived on the island, their ghostly presence still very evident in the linear lazy beds that everywhere run up the hills and valleys. The devastating results of the Great Famine, which lasted from 1845 to 1849, followed by eviction and emigration, reduced the population drastically. When the Congested Districts Board took over the island in 1895, paying the last landlord £5486, there were 692 people living there. The practice of the ancient Rundale system meant subdivisions of land into small uneconomic parcels "about as bad a mode as the mind of man could devise," according to a report. There was hardly any fishing. The Board intervened dramatically: 77 new farms were created, roads and almost eighty kilometres (fifty miles) of stone walls were built, and a fishing industry established. Tenancies were abolished, and families became owners of their own land.

The dwindling numbers could not be stopped, however, and throughout the twentieth century emigration has taken its inevitable toll. Today the population of Clare, numbering around a hundred and fifty, face changes that have affected other Irish islands. However, although they suffer from the decline of small-scale farming and a dependence on subsidies, it is hoped that the present decline in population has halted.

ACHILL

ACHILL

Achill is the largest and most westerly island not only off the Irish coast, but off Europe itself. It has an area of 14,760 hectares (57 square miles), including the smaller islands of Achill Beg and Inishbiggle. The climate here is generally mild with no frosts, but the island is windy and wet, and frequently covered with sea mists. The present population is nearly three thousand.

Rising between Clew Bay to the south and Blacksod Bay to the north, Achill's inverted L-shape contains a mountainous interior covered with heath and bog. The three dominant mountains are Slievemore (661 metres/2204 feet) a great quartzite cone shot with mica, Minawn (460 metres/1530 feet) and Croaghaun (658 metres/2192 feet), whose three-kilometre (two-mile) precipice drops into the sea. The sea cliffs of Achill look as if they have been sliced away by the Atlantic and are said to be the highest in Europe. There are numerous sandy beaches and mountain lakes. An unusual relict flora survives on the slopes of Croaghaun and Slievemore (which are technically known as nunataks), where the Ice Age did not reach. In recent years a new species has taken to the moist air and is to be found everywhere—gunnera, imported

from Asia, which looks like giant rhubarb.

Lloyd Praeger, who returned to the island again and again, wrote how "Achill, windswept and bare…with great gaunt brown mountains…and a wild coast hammered by the Atlantic waves on all sides but the east, has a strange charm which everybody feels but none can explain." Much of the charm derived from the remoteness and mystery of this large land mass at the far end of Mayo.

The first settlement on Achill has been dated to around 5000B.C. Ancient remains range from middens, cooking sites, stone circles, megaliths, Ogham stones, hut sites, cairns, and cashels to the more recent ruins of the medieval church of Kildavnet and the fifteenth-century tower house associated with Grace O'Malley.

In the eighteenth century there were no roads at all and a traveller like Arthur Young was deterred from making the short crossing from the mainland into the unknown. He could only report how "eagles abounded very much in carrying away lambs, poultry, etc., and they also catch the salmon." In the early nineteenth century ten to twelve Irish-speaking families lived here as tenants of the O'Donnell family. Subsequently Achill attracted sportsmen and their guns, since the

island's mild climate and remote situation drew huge quantities of migrating birds, such as swans, geese, and different species of wild duck, some of which were rare even in those days.

Over the mountains golden eagles and white-tailed sea eagles were often seen. The author of *Wild Sports of the West*, Robert Maxwell, hunted on Slievemore chasing the "pesty" birds, "flaunting themselves high above their eyrie with their brood and teaching the young birds some of their skills. The old birds tore up turfs from the mountainside, rose higher in the air, and dropped them for the young eagles to catch." The islanders found a source of income by scaling the cliffs in search of eggs belonging to "these splendid Arabs of the air." Some people had them as pets, like the naturalist William Pike, who lived on Achill and kept a tame eagle for 26 years, taken in 1854 as a young bird from its nest. (He also had a tame chough which roosted every night over the kitchen fireplace.)

Eagles were still flying over Achill when the Reverend Edward Nangle arrived in 1831, partly for health reasons and partly to take potatoes to the inhabitants, who were suffering from famine. Soon afterwards Nangle set about his self-appointed task to convert the islanders. Some considered him "a man of deep personal piety and animated with a burning zeal for the glory of God." "Like another Luther is Mr Nangle on Achill," wrote an admirer, "preaching twice a day against Popery, exposing the craft of the priest." But others considered that he took advantage of the bitter poverty of Achill's people.

In a land without walls or hedges, Nangle found an impoverished congregation that had

an unjust reputation of being thieves and murderers. In spite of furious opposition from the Catholic Church and the disapproval of witnesses and travellers such as the American missionary Asenath Nicholson, his Achill Mission was destined to change the island for ever.

He began by buying land from the bankrupt O'Donnell landowners and soon established a settlement around Dugort. Fields were drained, crops sown, and under the misty slopes of Slievemore an entire new village took shape. By the time of Asenath Nicholson's visit in the early 1840s, the white cabins, the infant school, the female school, and the dining hall in which a hundred orphans were fed, were in place. John Barrow illustrated Dugort, with its neat squares in front of the houses; it still looks very much the same except that the reclaimed land has gone wild. In 1839 a fine new hotel was opened that still attracts visitors.

Reluctant converts were made during the famine. By 1852 the colony was able to buy two-thirds of the island, which made Nangle the principal landlord. His proselytising activities invited concentrated opposition not only from the parish priest, Father Connolly, but from the formidable Archbishop MacHale of Tuam. For a time Nangle had to have an armed guard. Wrangling and the exchange of insults between Catholics and Protestants continued for many years; as late as 1878 Murray's *Handbook for Travellers in Ireland* went out of its way to warn the visitor of "a lack of religious charity which each party would do well to discard."

Things have ended better. St Thomas' Church, which was opened in 1854, still faces Slievemore and the little white houses. It has a plain interior with pinewood benches and a modest tablet commemorates the "Reverend Edward Nangle, Founder of the Achill Mission, who died September 9th, 1883 in the

TOP: The Deserted Village, of around ninety ruined cottages, with their stone gables surviving.
ABOVE LEFT: The common cotton grass, *Eriophorum angustifolium*, better known as bog cotton.
ABOVE RIGHT: The flowers of the bog bean, *Menyantes trifoliata*, appear in still waters in late spring.

83rd year of his age…." The visitors' book is filled with remarks like "inspiring" and "how peaceful!" Services are open to members of both religious communities.

An ironic twist to the Reverend Nangle's fiery sermons is that today the Catholic Church is still grumbling as people from all over Ireland are flocking to Achill to Christine Gallagher's House of Prayer in the former Convent of Mercy.

Another notorious nineteenth-century inhabitant of Achill was Captain Charles Boycott, who lived in Corrymore House, some distance from Keel. As a young man of 25 he arrived in Achill in 1857, leasing land from the Mission and staying 20 years before departing to become the agent for the Earl of Erne on his lands in Ballinrobe in Mayo. He is credited with introducing goats to the island. When Thomas Mason visited Achill in the early 1930s he met a man who remembered the man whose name gave a new word to the English language. "Sure," said he, "we had to run him out of Achill and I hear they ran him out of Mayo later on." I asked, "In what way was he a tyrant?" "Well," said my informant, "if ye spat on the yard he would fine ye. He was a terrible man."

It is unlikely that Boycott was associated with the best-known site on the island, the Deserted Village, which winds along a contour of the south-facing slope of Slievemore. No one knows exactly what combination of poverty, hardship, emigration, and eviction caused the population to leave or when exactly it was abandoned during the second half of the nineteenth century. Amid an elaborate alignment of lazy beds there are about ninety houses, most aligned north-south. Similar dwellings were described by Edward Newman in 1838: "huts which a good deal resemble those of the Esquimaux Indians…without

RIGHT: Young harpers at Achill's annual music festival continue a thousand-year-old tradition.

chimneys or windows and the roof seems continuous with the walls; the interior is generally divided and is tenanted by men, women, children, pigs and poultry, and often goats and cows."

The German writer Heinrich Böll, who loved Achill, described these crumbling lines of stone-gabled one-roomed cabins as "the skeleton of a village, shuddering in its struc-

ture…all that was not stone eaten away from rain, sun and wind—and from time, which patiently dripped over all: twenty-four great drops per day…."

On Achill there was a time warp. Life continued to be exceptionally hard for islanders, many of whom went each year to Scotland as "tatie hokies" or potato pickers. Old traditions changed slowly. Above the Deserted Village are remains of the small oval-shaped

booley houses made from stone and sods; a bog road linked the Deserted Village with Dooagh for the summer booley season which began on the first of May. This form of seasonal trans-humance—taking livestock from lowland villages to the mountain slopes—observed by Newman in 1838, continued on Achill until the 1940s—the last place in Ireland where the practice occurred.

Achill began to open up to outsiders in 1888 when the first iron swivel bridge formed a link with the mainland. No longer did islanders have to rely on the ferry or the walk across the sand to their homes. At the same time as the bridge was built, the construction of a railway line from Westport to Achill Sound invited discovery. Here was an island easy of access where old customs and traditions survived. There were specific attractions like the famous seal caves; one of them, the "Priest's Cave," is said to be the haunt of a rare species of sea otter, nearly black with paler colouring beneath its throat. There were the famous cliffs—nowadays people hang glide off them—the unusual flora and Lough Nakeeroge, Ireland's lowest corrie lake.

There was the ever-changing light, with no two days quite the same. The painter Paul Henry discovered it and his life was transformed. In 1912 he came to Achill for two weeks and stayed eight years. He made Achill known to the world with his pictures, some of which were used as railway posters but brought him little money. He painted fishermen in bawneen and women in scarlet skirts and shawls, every bit as handsome as those on Aran. Today his pictures of thatched cottages, blue mountains, and cabbage-shaped cumulus clouds have never been so popular. Nor has Achill itself. The changes have been rapid. As recently as 1976 a guide book could recommend the island as "an ideal holiday resort for seekers after solitude." Who can say how much caravan parks, new hotels, and tourist homes have improved the island?

INISHMURRAY

INISHMURRAY

PREVIOUS PAGE: Looking north over Inishmurray to the coast of Donegal. The island boasts a concentration of massive stone buildings: beehive huts, churches, and other landmarks associated with the monastery founded by St Molaise.
LEFT: The pear-shaped dry stone cashel contains four walled partitions and a wealth of monastic buildings, including a small church.
ABOVE: There is no harbour, and access is by a pier at the east end, visible here. Many visitors now land by helicopter.

The name of this island, six kilometres (four miles) off Sligo at the entrance to Donegal Bay, derives from Inis Muirdeach, honouring Muirdeach, Bishop of Killala, one of the Uí Néill and a descendant of Niall of the Nine Hostages, better known as St Molaise. After having been ordained by St Patrick, he founded the monastery on Inishmurray, much of which is still there. Nowhere else in Ireland is there such a wealth of early Christian remains in such a small area.

Almost flat, rising to a maximum height of 21 metres (70 feet) with cliffs and rocky shores, Inishmurray is one-and-a-half kilometres (a mile) long by three-quarters-of-a kilometre (half-a-mile) wide. It is said that during the Second World War a British destroyer mistook it for a German U-boat and fired off a torpedo, shaking the inhabitants in their beds. On my first visit I saw it from a helicopter and it looked like a floating green leaf. Its geology is perverse: over on the Sligo coast the rock is limestone, while here it is composed of sandstone.

There is no harbour and no easy access, only a pier at the east end. In 1936 when Thomas Mason departed in a storm, the skipper of the boat admonished his crew: "Will ye pull—'tis like women ye are pulling! Mind that mast and stop talking!" and to the terrified passengers: "Will ye stay quiet?"

Perhaps the sea was rough when St Molaise first came over. The discovery in 1938 of an early food vessel indicates a settlement before his time going back to around 200B.C., and there is undoubtedly a wealth of prehistoric remains yet to be discovered. But history begins with the arrival of St Molaise and his monks at a provisional date of A.D.520.

A haunting oak statue of Inishmurray's patron saint wearing his monk's robes stands in the National Museum in Dublin. It is generally recognised as dating from the thirteenth century, which makes it older than any similar statue in Ireland. St Molaise has no arms, since they were hacked off by a religious zealot named Loftus Jones—who went mad and tried to bite off his own shoulders. The "disgusting idol" was thrown in the sea, but miraculously retrieved, only to fall victim to love and veneration instead of hate. Islanders chipped off small pieces of the statue to send to their relatives, until a priest, Father O'Crehan, intervened, and holy medals were substituted.

Another exiled relic of the saint is the beautiful *Soisceal Molaise*, St Molaise's

Shrine, intricately worked with metal, which is kept a short distance from the Museum at the Royal Hibernian Academy (who paid £46 for it back in 1860). Molaise's crosier and hand bell are in a collection at Alnwick Castle in Northumberland. For years the bell was lost until it was traced by Dr Cormac Bourke in 1981, who discovered it had been acquired by an antiquarian Duke of Northumberland; for good measure the crosier was also there.

According to legend St Columcille also came to Inishmurray, and his presence dominates the island almost as much as his brother saint Molaise. Columcille is said to have come to the island for a sin he had committed during "the Battle of the Books." A dispute with St Finian over the transcription of the Bible led to the death of many of their followers. In remorse he journeyed to Inishmurray and placed himself under the discipline of St Molaise, who sent him on his missionary crusade to Iona. The first of the 16 stations around the island is called *Leachta*

Cholmcille, the memorial altar of Columcille.

What the monks built under the direction of St Molaise and his successors during the sixth and seventh centuries are contained inside a massive dry-stone cashel whose walls are four metres (12 feet) thick and five metres (15 feet) high. There are three ground-level entrances, wall chambers, and defensive stepping within the walls. It is possible that the huge enclosure predated the monks who adapted it. When in A.D.807 the Vikings raided the island and burned it, we do not know if the monks were grateful for the protective walling. Almost a thousand years later, in 1888, the Board of Works repaired the walls and created the southern entrance. A local tradition asserts that the cashel was damaged some time during the eighteenth century when it was used as a target by gunboats of the Royal Navy.

Within this pear-shaped fortress are four walled partitions crowded with monastic buildings. They include three intact beehive

huts and three pillar stones, together with 27 souterrains that run underground. In the largest enclosure is *Teach Molaise*, St Molaise's House, a tiny building three metres by two-and-three-quarter metres (nine foot by eight foot) which the islanders used as their church. Until they left in 1948, St Molaise's statue stood here at the junction of two altars. A low stone bench on the southern wall is called *Leaba Molaise* or Molaise's Bed.

Other buildings here include a clochann or beehive hut known as *Tory Bhrennell*—the Schoolhouse—because it contains a stone bench, and the larger *Teach na Teine*—the House of Fire—because it contains a central hearth thought to be the monks' kitchen.

There are two further churches within the cashel, one of which is the *Teampall na bhfear*, the Men's Church, where men were buried. The women were buried outside the walls at *Teampall na mBan*, the Women's Church. This unique segregation suggests that there may have been women on Inishmurray before the monks abandoned the island probably some time in the twelfth century. What was their role? The presence of lay communities and the position of women living adjacent to hermetic monastic settlements remains a mystery. Also, outside the wall on the north side of the cashel is an ancient sweat house, an Irish version of a Turkish bath with a well nearby where bathers could dowse themselves after steaming.

From the earliest years of the monastery Inishmurray was a place of pilgrimage, and around the island are 11 stations for pilgrims making their clockwise rounds. They are marked by altars, cross-inscribed stones, memorials, wells, and other structures, some looming right over the sea. Near the Men's

LEFT: Around the edges of the island the ancient pilgrim route is marked by altars and crosses.
ABOVE RIGHT: Deserted houses on the south-eastern shore. The last inhabitants left in 1948.

Church stands a cross pillar with holes in to help pregnant women raise themselves after they had prayed there. One inscribed stone from the monastic graveyard, which has now been removed for safekeeping, is said to be unique in Western Europe for its combination of vernacular and Latin: *Or do Muirdeach Hu chomacain hic dormit*—Pray for Muirdeach, scion of Comacan, who lies here.

Perhaps the most singular station is the Clocha Breaca, an altar containing a number of round stones each inscribed with a cross collected between two cross-inscribed uprights. Two stones resemble bottles hollowed at their ends with a stone fitting like a cork. There used to be 50, but many of the more portable, like Muirdeach's gravestone, have been taken away to protect them from thieves coming to the deserted island. Islanders called them speckled or blessed stones, but these are the cursing stones, which could be used after careful preparation (including a three-day fast). If you cursed your enemy wrongly, the curse would rebound on you. During the Second World War an Englishwoman used the stones to curse Hitler.

Other less lurid beliefs lingered over the centuries. St Molaise rightly banished rats. Three drops of water from one of the two holy wells sprinkled on the sea would calm it. These wells were not for drinking; if anyone took a sip, a small lizard known as a "man keeper" would jump into his mouth. If a man or woman was buried in the wrong cemetery, the coffin would move by itself by night

to the one that corresponded with their sex. A sod of turf placed on the hearth of the House of Fire in the correct manner would light spontaneously.

St Molaise and his monks and the traditions and rituals they inspired dominated the lives of the people who came after them.

Nowhere else in Ireland is there such a wealth of early Christian remains in such a small area

To live on such visible holy ground inspired a particularly intense devotion to religion. Up until 1948 islanders carefully followed the pattern day, walking from one station to another. On Sundays the population would gather inside Teach Molaise and pray and recite the rosary kneeling before the two altars, the grave statue of St Molaise looking down. Since there was no resident priest, the ceremony would be timed to coincide with Sunday Mass said on the mainland.

Life on this bare spot, inaccessible for much of the year, was never easy. When Thomas Mason paid his visit in 1936, and less

than a hundred people lived here, he began a description with a list of inadequacies. No harbours, no roads, no clergy, no police, no magistrate, no doctor, no shop, no rates, no rats, and no public house.

For the men of Inishmurray the routine of fishing and farming their poor soil in patchwork fields was augmented by a lively trade in poteen. Inishmurray poteen was famous; a special contingent of *gardaí* (police) was organised to chase after Inishmurray's illicit brew. The first glass of every distillation was given to the fairies. There are always reasons given why islands are abandoned. Sometimes it is a great storm like the tempest that made the inhabitants of Iniskea depart. On Inishmurray one reason offered for the final evacuation in 1948 was a shortage of sugar during the Emergency which prevented the making of poteen.

But as on so many other islands it was the corrosive effects of poverty and isolation that made this fervent little community abandon the holy places. The population had peaked to around 102 people in 1880; a census of 1926 gave the number as 74, but when the leave-taking came this had been reduced to 46. Today the ruined houses face the mainland.

Left to itself, the low-lying bleak island with its cliffs and rocky shores has been officially designated a bird sanctuary. Barnacle geese, Arctic terns, storm petrels, and eider ducks are among the birds that call into Inishmurray. And St Molaise's wonderful legacy remains—an Irish Angkor Wat.

TORY

TORY

PREVIOUS PAGE: Puffins,
which belong to the auk
family, nest in holes or
burrows on steep slopes
overlooking the sea. The
colony on Tory is one of
only about twenty
around the Irish coast.
LEFT: Along the wild
coast the sea has
hollowed out caves and
strange rock formations
from the hard quartzite.
These caves are at the
east end of the island
beneath Balor's fort.
ABOVE: Tory, whose
length can be seen here
from the east end, is
bare and treeless.

Tory, 12 kilometres (eight miles) off Donegal, is the most northerly of the inhabited islands of Ireland. Less than five kilometres (three miles) long and a kilometre (three-quarters of a mile) at its widest point, bare and windswept, it often seems as inhospitable as an iceberg. All along its northern edge hard resistant quartzites have formed into terrifying sea cliffs. From this massive line of *toraigh,* which give the island its name—the Place of Towers—the land tapers to the south, where a peneplain on less resistant granite slopes more gently. Here is the thin covering of turf bog, which the islanders have been scraping away for hundreds of years, and some arable fields, which are at the mercy of westerly winds. In the days when the islanders depended on farming, the salt spray blowing everywhere was always a menace, although crops were protected to some extent by stone walls. Late spring and cool summers meant that harvests came late. Today the only tree on Tory is an overgrown bush of some wind- and sea-resistant nature which stands outside the priest's house—so its preservation may be miraculous....

Belonging more to the Atlantic than to Ireland, the people of Tory maintained a wholly Gaelic culture with customs that dated back for centuries. They still speak their own brand of Gaelic. While much ancient tradition had vanished on the mainland or "the Country," here they kept the Rundale system of farming derived from the Celts. People lived together in settlements and went out to their fields, which were arranged in strips—each farmer would own one here, and one there. These striped fields are still to be seen all over the island. Long after the people on the mainland had abandoned outmoded farming practices, Tory islanders continued to use the flail for threshing, while their ponies and donkeys pulled the wheel-less slide car. They fished the wild Atlantic in tiny coracles similar to Boyne coracles, which can still be seen. Their archaic social structures fascinated the anthropologist Robin Fox, who in 1978 published a classic account of a unique community which he described as "a people of the Celtic fringe."

A visit to the island used to be a daunting ordeal. In 1835 the dogged Gaelic scholar John O'Donovan wrote: "I have given up the idea of landing on Tory for many reasons, amongst the strongest of which is that I might, in this stormy season, be detained for a month upon it without being able to get back to the continent of Tir-Connell." More

than a century later the Automobile Association Guide of 1976 warned: "A person visiting this isolated place in poor weather is liable to be stranded on the island for days."

Before the introduction of a new ferry service in 1992, there were many occasions when Tory was inaccessible. Often during the 1960s and '70s Johnny Dixon's mail boat, a half decker fitted with an unreliable engine and a tattered brown sail, could not face the strong westerly winds, the rolling waters of the Atlantic and the powerful current flowing along the island's southern coast. In 1972 Kevin Crossley-Holland was told that Tory was a place where "no one would ask to go." He found the crossing from Magheraroarty, "in the true sense of the word, terrible. The boat began to kick and buck as soon as we had backed off the pier, and freezing spray sheets flew over the bows...." So fierce are the storms that as recently as the winter of 1974 Tory was isolated for eight weeks; ten families immediately decided to leave their bleak home for good.

The new ferry launched in 1992 is a stout vessel, and sails regularly—in summer up to five times a day. Recently, I was blessed with good weather and the crossing took less than an hour. We passed the islands of Inishbofin, Inishdoney, and Inishbeg, and chugged out to sea where Tory waited, long and narrow. At the eastern end were the knife-edged cliffs of Tor Mór extending from the Doon peninsula; at the west end the lighthouse. In 1827 Caesar Otway described the island as "rising out of the deep like a castellated city, lofty towers,

"...lofty towers, church spires, battlements, batteries and bastions apparently presented themselves...."

CAESAR OTWAY, 1835

church spires, battlements, batteries and bastions apparently presented themselves, so strangely varied and so fantastically deceptive were its cliffs."

The ferry entered Camusmore Bay and approached the small West Town, which looks like nowhere else in Ireland. At the turn of the century the old cabins in which cattle shared the hearth during the winter months clustered around St Columcille's tower. Then came the clachán-style houses built by the Congested Districts Board, with sash windows, wooden floors and slate roofs. The tower, of which 17 metres (57 feet) remain, built of rounded beach stones and rough blocks of granite, looks like no other round tower. It could be a minaret, and the whitewashed houses could belong to a Moorish village. Cocks and hens scuffle their feathers in the dust, an old lady arrives to do her shopping at the one store on the forklift of a tractor, while the priest walks past surrounded by a pack of dogs. Above the small harbour with its new pier—courtesy of European Community funds—is the T-shaped Tau cross made of thick mica slate, and nearby the remains of the two churches and monastery founded by St Columcille in the sixth century.

To the West Town belongs not only the tower, but the church, the priest's house (with its tree), the hostel, the hotel, the pub, and all that forms the heart of island life. The East Village, situated a short distance away, has the same "Board" houses and the same view of Donegal.

Less than ten years ago the islanders still lived by farming and fishing, backed up with Gaeltacht grants and flotsam from the sea. Sheep and cattle were kept on the thin strips of land which supported just enough grass to

TOP: The Round Tower is a remnant of St Columcille's monastery, founded in the sixth century.
ABOVE: Abandoned winch gear at Port an Duin.

feed them. The old ways were maintained at a cost; the cottages were small, many crumbling or abandoned. The roads were unmade, with stinking open drains beside them. (But you are assured that, like Inishmurray, there are no rats on Tory.)

In 1936 Thomas Mason observed the primitive implements then in use. Ploughs were home-made, composed of wood shod with iron retrieved from wrecks; harrows were made of wood and iron bolts from ships. Shipwrecks provided a valuable source of fuel and sometimes food. A few months before Mason's visit a wrecked ship provided the islanders with enough flour for a year.

There is no lime; to obtain it, shells and limpets used to be burned in a hollow square of turf. Fuel was a constant problem as for centuries the islanders burned the peaty sod which formed their pastures. Today two old brothers are the only people on Tory who dig the turf and their little stacks are to be seen round the East Village. The rest burn coal or use gas, both brought from the mainland.

In the 1970s there were plans for full-scale evacuation, after which the abandoned island would be turned into a firing range or a prison. With a reprieve the community took on a new lease of life. Today the ferry brings in a steady trickle of tourists, some of whom stay in the new hotel. The island is sucked into the welfare system of grants which has brought running water and electricity. Television is there for the long winter evenings, with many houses fitted with dishes to receive satellite programmes.

The fact that fishing and agriculture have both suddenly become superfluous to the island

ABOVE LEFT: Poet and fisherman Eamonn Dooley Rodgers, in about 1900.
ABOVE RIGHT: The King of Tory, Patsy Dan Rodgers, with one of his paintings.
BELOW: A sea arch on the cliffs on the north-eastern coastline, Balor's country.

lifestyle may be considered a cost. I was told that there were three cows left among the unkempt fields, shorthorns, a breed now threatened with extinction. I saw one cow cropping the long grass, a number of donkeys and a handful of sheep. Milk, together with potatoes and cabbages, comes over daily from the mainland. The day I asked in the shop for potatoes, I was offered a well-known American brand of rice instead. Vegetable gardens have vanished, together with the cows. Only the hens are still there, and those staying at the hostel are woken by cock crow.

For decades the artist Derek Hill spent his summers on Tory and did much of his best work from his rudimentary hut at the east end—portraits of the islanders and powerful landscapes of the spirit-level length of Tory and towering cliffs pounded by silver seas. It was Hill who created the "school" of Tory Island painters. The best of these artists by far was the first; James Dixon had a vision, and much of the wildness and magic of his island makes its way into his simple paintings. Although he has been a hard act to follow, the primitive charm of such artists as Patsy Dan Rodgers, the King of Tory, and Ruairi Rodgers, has earned them international recognition. The Rodgers are inheritors of the tradition granted to the Duggan family and the privilege of calling themselves Kings of the island.

Beyond the East Village and Doon harbour is the headland of Tor Mór with its cliffs and Anvil Rock. Here is Balor's country. Tory was the stronghold of the Formorians, among whom were Balor of the Evil Eye, the Lord of Darkness, and his grandson Lugh, the Lord of Light, who eventually blinded his wicked old grandfather. Choughs, sea birds, and rabbits inhabit the area around Dún Bhalair, Balor's quadrivallate promontory fort. The west end, dominated by the lighthouse, is broader and flatter than the east, although here too the cliffs are huge and eaten out by the destructive force of the sea into caverns and grottoes and strange rock formations. In a little bay below the nearby cemetery I watched the biggest seals I have ever seen lounging on the rocks. They could have been Balor's children.

RATHLIN

RATHLIN

Twenty years ago I crossed to Rathlin in a cattle boat, the *Iona*, which had deposited cattle at Ballycastle and was shipping bags of coal and bottles of vodka back to the island. I was the only passenger. The 45-minute crossing over the 11-kilometre (seven-mile) stretch of water, whose currents are known as the *Brochán,* or Boiling Porridge Pot, and the whirlpool *Slough na Morra,* or the Swallow of the Sea, passed without incident. I knew that at other times bad weather and powerful currents not only isolated Rathlin but provided a danger to ships. To add to the dangers, this sound is the foggiest place on the coast of Ireland.

The men of Rathlin had a prayer: "May God be good and send a shipwreck," which He did frequently. In the pub are displayed some of the name boards of ships that went down. Among those buried in the cemetery of St Thomas' Church are three nameless sailors, "known unto God," drowned in the First World War, and one Elizabeth Browning, cast ashore from a ship called the *Cambria*: "Her Sun Went Down While it was Yet Day." No wonder there are three lighthouses.

Other voyagers in the neighbouring seas who have been unlucky were two MacDonnells drowned on their way to Scotland. The sea took Brecain, son of Niall of the Nine hostages, and his entire fleet.

The German traveller Johannes Kohl gazed at the white line of cliffs from his inn at Ballycastle that seemed so near. "While contemplating Rathlin I thought of Shakespeare's *Tempest* and the island of the banished Duke Prospero." Enchantment is associated with the seas to the north, towards the Mull of Kintyre, which are the waters of Moyle where the children of Lir spent 300 years as swans.

Man has braved the dangers of the sound for 6000 years, as traces of Stone-Age settlements indicate. In the townland of Brockley axes were manufactured from an exceptionally tough rock called porcellanite. By 2500B.C., until they were superseded by bronze, porcellanite axes from Rathlin were exported to England, Scotland, and other parts of Ireland.

Rathlin, or to give its ancient name, *Raghery,* the Isle of Sheep, or perhaps the Isle of Ships, is mentioned by Ptolemy and Pliny who called it welcome Ricnia. Vikings pillaged the monastery here. But its long bloody history is largely dictated by the fact that it is a stepping stone between Ireland and Scotland. From Rue Point you can look across to the Mull of Kintyre only 24 kilometres (15 miles) away, and on a clear day you can pick

"While contemplating Rathlin I thought…of the island of the banished Duke Prospero"

JOHANNES KOHL, 1844

out Scottish farmhouses. The dual nature of the islanders was observed by Thomas Mason: "It is hard to realise that one is in Ireland, the Scottish coast appearing almost as near as the mainland of Ireland; and indeed…their accent is a cross between Northern Irish and lowland Scots."

The islanders had a curse among themselves: "May Ireland be your hinder end." To be sent to the mainland was considered a punishment. In 1816 Anne Plumptree observed how "the inhabitants are not less attached to their dreary and desolate home than those that dwell under the most auspicious and benign sun."

Pre-eminent among Scottish visitors was Robert Bruce, king of Scotland, who took refuge here in 1306. Did he really hide in a

RIGHT: Young fulmars at West Lighthouse. In the past, the men of Rathlin made perilous descents down the cliff faces to collect sea birds' eggs.
BELOW LEFT: One of the many small island loughs.
BELOW RIGHT: The basalt stacks are great favourites with sea birds such as razorbills and kittiwakes.

cave where he observed the tenacity of a spider repeatedly trying to weave its web?

There is more historical evidence of two massacres. In 1575 islanders were slaughtered on orders of the Earl of Essex by John Norris and Francis Drake—scant remains of the castle they battered with their guns have survived. A bloody episode took place in 1642, when a large force of Campbells landed on Rathlin and took their revenge on the MacDonnells. The hill to the east of the harbour where the MacDonnell women watched the massacre of their menfolk is *Cnoc na Screedlin*, the Hill of Screaming.

Rathlin is shaped like a boomerang or a letter "L," of which one arm going west to east is six kilometres (four miles) long, the other from north to south four-and-a-half kilometres (three miles). While compiling the Down Survey in the seventeenth century, William Petty compared it to "an Irish stockin, the toe of which pointeth to the main lande." Most of the fields, cottages, and hills rest on top of 25 kilometres (16 miles) of towering cliffs, which make up 90 per cent of the coast line. The deep base of chalk which edges them has been compared to a white pie frill, and their contrasting colouring to a magpie. Sea birds nest in huge numbers, particularly at the west end at the Kebble nature reserve, where cliffs tumble into the water in the form of "stacks," providing nesting space to guillemots, kittiwakes, razorbills, and fulmars. In the past the men of Rathlin were expert crags men, making perilous descents to collect eggs. All over the island wading birds are attracted to numerous little reedy lakes, the largest of which is Lough Ushet at the southern end near Rue Point.

There are the remains of a monastic settlement at Knockans, including an old sweat house, which may have been converted from an older beehive hut. Beside the Neolithic axe factory at Brockley is a prehistoric mud fort. Behind the village in Church Bay there is a standing stone.

The monks were here; the monastic foundation of St Congall of Bangor dated to about 580 is on the site of the present church of St Thomas. Other early Christian traces have all but vanished, except for bases of circular huts on a hill in the townland of Knockans.

The sea caverns in the cliffs, which are only accessible by boat, include Bruce's cave below the East Lighthouse where he teased the arachnid, which, as Winston Churchill pointed out, is the most celebrated spider in history. Above on the cliffs is "Bruce's Castle," a few pieces of crumbling masonry dramatically positioned on a rock stack 24 metres (80 feet) high, more properly associated with the Norman John de Courcy than with the Scottish chieftain.

The three lighthouses make landmarks for walking. Because of its angled shape, the explorer is constantly returning to the island's elbow at Church Bay, which is the only proper village. On no other Irish island is there such a mix of buildings. Where else would you get two churches, Protestant and Catholic, coastguard houses, and an imposing landlord's house?

Landlords who acquired Irish islands were principally absentees, relying on agents to collect rent. On Rathlin different circumstances prevailed. In 1747 the island was bought by a clergyman, the Rev. John Gage, whose son Robert built the Manor House. For 200 years the Gages were virtual kings of Rathlin. While the majority of islanders were Catholic their "proprietors" were Protestant. In 1884 the *Parliamentary Gazetteer* described the Rev. George Gage as "completely Lord of the island who banishes his subjects to the continent of Ireland for misconduct or repeated offences against the law." Whenever the Reverend himself journeyed to the mainland he was rowed by a liveried crew in striped blue-and-white jerseys.

The Gages may have acted like despots, but in many ways they were good to their people, particularly during the famine. In the late nineteenth century Robert Gage provided his people with coal, erected a lime kiln, and started a boat-building industry. In 1973 the Manor House, a long grey building in the Georgian style with gardens and numerous outhouses, was taken over by the local community. Until recently Rathliners were Gaelic-speaking, which must have been a further reason for division with their landlord. The language only petered out in the 1930s.

The island's population has dwindled from

over a thousand before the famine to just over a hundred today, living by farming, fishing, and tourism. In summer a festival week brings the people over and a regatta includes the Killarney-to-Rathlin yacht race. There is a guest house, and the Richard Branson Activity Centre, backed by the grateful balloonist whose balloon came down in the nearby Waters of Moyle. A modern ferry takes tourists over daily all year unless the weather is terrible. In short, a strong community spirit is evident, and the people insist that Rathlin has a future and the decline has been stopped.

LAMBAY

LAMBAY

I have a cracked blue-and-white bowl which was retrieved by divers off the Tayleur Rocks north-west of Lambay. In January 1854 the *Tayleur*, an emigrant ship, set off from Liverpool to Melbourne. She was tacking across the Irish sea in foul weather when, too late, she sighted Lambay and struck the rocks. Six hundred perished; a handful of survivors aided by coastguards managed to reach safety. While these were being fed oatmeal and potatoes by the steward of Lord Malahide, it is said many of the bodies washed up on the shore were robbed by the islanders.

Lord Talbot de Malahide was one of a series of owners of this east-coast island which is located 11 kilometres (seven miles) north of Howth Head and three miles (four-and-three-quarter kilometres) south east of Rush. An air passenger can get a quick glimpse of the square mile of rock, heather, and turf just before his plane descends to Dublin airport. Lambay's long chequered history has included many of the usual protagonists—Neolithic man, monks, Vikings and pirates. An intriguing discovery in 1927 was of various buried Roman artifacts, including a cylinder of pink wax.

More certain than the Romans in their association are the Vikings, who in A.D.795, with a fleet of 120 ships, made their first attack on Ireland from the island, which they later used as a base. The old name of Rechru was changed to the Danish *Lambay*—Lamb Island.

There is no trace of the monastery that is thought to have been founded by St Columcille in the sixth century but which the Vikings may have destroyed. Nor is anything to be seen of a chantry chapel authorised in 1337. By that time the Normans had long been in charge; in 1184 Lambay was granted by Prince John, then Earl of Moreton, to John Comyn, who became Archbishop of Dublin in 1134.

In the Middle Ages the island was home to pirates, and according to a protest of 1467 "a receptacle for the King's enemies... Spaignardes, homes de Frances and Scottes." In 1500 the Prior of St Patrick's of Holmpatrick claimed that pirates sheltered in the havens and creeks of Lambay. In Tudor times Lambay became less safe for pirates. John Tiptoft, Earl of Worcester, built a fortress granted to him by the Irish Parliament, presumably after the Dissolution. In 1534 a pirate named Brodie, presumably a "Scotte," was chased from Lambay to Drogheda by the

ships of Sir William Skeffington which "bowged him so that he ran his vessel a-land."

For a short time the incoming English used Lambay as a naval base to assemble warships and troopships. Then it was deserted or "wast." One John Challoner leased "his little kingdom of Lambay" to mine it for "marbles of rare beauty"—the porphyry and green-stone which is found there. During the Williamite wars Lambay became an island prison for Jacobite prisoners captured at the Battle of Aughrim, many of whom starved to death. It passed into the hands of the Usher family, which owned it until 1804, after which followed various owners. A community lived there—at the time of the *Tayleur* shipwreck there are said to have been 100 families on the island.

In 1903 Cecil Baring, a wealthy English banker, was enjoying a holiday in Munich when he came across an advertisement in *The Field*—"Irish Island for sale"—and promptly bought Lambay. On a visit to the National Library of Ireland to seek out information about his new acquisition, Baring met Lloyd Praeger, who suggested that here was an opportunity to make a detailed study of Lambay's natural habitat. The island's origins have fascinated geologists, being the stump of an ancient volcano marked by the slope to the north-east, rising to the conical hill of Knockban. Millions of years ago lava of the type called andesitic broke through the earth's crust and poured out, covering an area far larger than the current area of Lambay. Three sides of the island have cliffs and stacks

that are inhabited by sea birds and caves that are home to grey seals; only to the east does it slope down to a beach and a harbour.

Between 1905 and 1906, according to Praeger, 20 scientific experts "ransacked the island from end to end." They found three worms, a mite, and a bristletail which were new to science, "twelve other animals were new to the Britannic fauna; and between eighty and ninety animals and plants were hitherto unrecorded from Ireland." This survey of Lambay not only had the profound effect of preserving the island as a wildlife

ABOVE: Formal planting was achieved on Lambay by Gertrude Jekyll, collaborating with Sir Edwin Lutyens.
RIGHT: Cecil Baring commissioned Lutyens to turn his island into a rich man's paradise.

sanctuary, but also gave Praeger the impetus for the more detailed survey of Clare Island, which he organised a few years later.

Baring was astute enough to employ the skills of the young unknown Edwin Lutyens at the outset of a career that would establish him among the foremost of English architects. Lutyens first came to Lambay in 1905,

but did not start serious work until 1907. He began with Tiptoft's sixteenth-century castle, making the roof weatherproof with grey pantiles brought over from Skerries, and putting a frieze of high Irish stepped battlements around the tower.

Lutyens built or adapted other buildings with a simple clarity of design. Whenever possible he used local or sympathetic material. The new buildings, with their pantile roofs and dormer windows, were assembled with the porphyry found on the island—stone with a coppery-green tinge, or copper-brown with feldspar crystals. The quoins are of old red sandstone and pale limestone from the mainland, which is also used for the windowsills. The walls of the old castle were covered with grey "haule," a kind of thick

pebbledash, and new work in thick mortar that covered the stone.

The main garden, drawn up to the design of Gertrude Jekyll, is round, divided into compartments like the slices of a cake. One critic, A. S. G. Butler, defined its magic as the "replay of little walled spaces within that great bounding circle ... They are almost like large roofless rooms."

Although she never visited the island, Miss Jekyll and Lutyens were already forming a partnership that associated their names like those of Gilbert and Sullivan. Planting, which took many years in the face of Lambay's winds, included magnolias, hydrangeas, hanging creepers, and herbaceous plants. Pillars found in the farm buildings were used for a pergola, one of Lutyens' favourite features. The provision of a curtain wall with a fine oak rampart gate and a raised walkway draped with cotoneaster, escallonia, and buckthorn helped to protect house and garden from the winds. It also gave it a far more fortified look than it had ever shown in the time of pirates.

There is a home farm and the wildlife has

multiplied, including the grey seals, peregrines, shelduck, shearwaters, and puffins that have taken over burrows of rabbits wiped out by myxamatosis. A large herd of fallow deer still roams the rocks and heather. At one time Baring had a zoo on the island with chamois, moufflon, and rheas.

Praeger's description of the castle on Lambay as "a very delightful modern residence" falls far short of conveying the delights of such a harmonious set of buildings. The complex included the rebuilding of the north side with a new block for kitchen quarters, various outbuildings including a boathouse, a Doric-style chapel, and the White House, designed for the daughter of Baring, by now Lord Revelstoke, in the 1930s.

Lutyens' final contribution to Lambay was the altar tomb to Lord Revelstoke and his wife, located under the ramparts. As much as the architect's romantic vision, "the visual poem that is Lambay" (in the words of Christopher Hussey) owes its expression to the rich man who purchased it on impulse and, together with his wife, devoted his life to overseeing its transformation. It always comes as a surprise that there is none of the Celtic vision here—Baring was in no way influenced by the ideas arising from the new Celtic enthusiasms that were changing the face of Ireland just across the sea. He taught his wife Greek so that she could read aloud Homer's account of Ulysses' return after the Trojan War, Ithaca was always on his mind, and looking at Lutyens' unique poetic creation, one is made aware that in spite of the Irish tower which he designed, Lambay is a foreign place. Only its tranquillity and the cries of its thousands of sea birds seem to link it with other Irish islands.

There are no roads or cars and Lambay preserves a sanity of its own by ignoring the tourist hordes. It is still owned by the family whose forebear saw the advertisement of an Irish island for sale.

IRELAND'S EYE

IRELAND'S EYE

Looking from Howth across the short divide of sea, the island that forms a buffer to the harbour floats magically beyond the busy streets of the village and distant Dublin. The strange craggy shape—the combination of a wedge-shaped mass of quartzite resting on beds of slate—seems top-heavy, with huge 90-metre (300-foot) cliffs which rise on its north side.

Statistics relating to Ireland's Eye are sparse:

Situation: 1.6 kilometres (one mile) north of Howth Peninsula
Area: 1.3 square kilometres (half a square mile)
Population: zero

The name is a meaningless corruption of *Inish Ereann*—the island of a woman called Eire or Eira. When the Danes renamed it they changed the Irish termination *Inis*, an island, for the Danish *oe*. In due course *Ereann* (of Eire) became *Eireann* (of Ireland). To add to the linguistic confusion the Latin version of its Gaelic name, Inis Mac Nessan, appears as *Insula Filiorum Nessani*, the Island of the Sons of Nessan, in a Bull of Pope Alexander III to St Laurence O'Toole, Archbishop of Dublin, in whose diocese the island lay.

For the thousands of visitors, mainly Dubliners, who make the short journey, the island's fame is less to do with any half-forgotten hermits than with an opportunity to escape for an hour or two. Open boats like *The Little Flower* or *The Angelus Bell* will take you on the 15-minute crossing. Immediately, the stresses of city life vanish and there is that special silence of deserted islands broken only by the scream of sea birds and the crash of waves. Few modern cities have such a sanctuary so near.

On the east side a rocky stack known as Puck's Rock was cleft from the cliffs, it is said, by the Devil; from the sea it looks like the helmet of a Roman soldier. Here is Ireland's newest gannetry, which began with a few birds who nested here in 1989. There are now several hundred and the number is rising. Soaring and diving overhead they indulge in one of the most beautiful of avian flights. Cormorants are also to be seen in huge numbers on the water or standing on rocks drying out their wings. Other birds include kitti-wakes, guillemots, razorbills, and the odd puffin, although the visitor on a day's outing will be lucky to see the bird, which Victorian ornithologists called the sea parrot. The greylag geese which flock here in winter can be seen from the mainland grazing the west slopes.

The landing is near the Martello Tower, built to the instructions of the Duke of York in 1803 as a fortification against a French invasion. Such towers were placed all around Dublin Bay; this one is mirrored by one on Howth harbour, although its particular stumpy design is associated with the tower on Dalkey Island, which also has a ruined church. Scattery Island is another fortified

sacred site abandoned to nature and God. Lloyd Praeger pointed out that the towers and ancient churches found so often together "are emblematic of the monuments found all over Ireland, representing piety and war."

Past the crescent-shaped sandy beach, a climb over sandy soil dotted with rabbit holes winds through bracken and leads to a summit where the visitor looks back to the wide panorama of Howth, its castle and marina and north Dublin's lines of bungalows and houses. To the north you can often see the

Mountains of Mourne some 80 kilometres (50 miles) away. Sometimes among the modern yachts a Howth five-metre (17-foot) yacht will pass by—one of the world's oldest surviving one-design keel boat class of racing yacht. To the east, smudged across the horizon in a dark blue line, is the bulk of Lambay.

The ruin of a small oratory, Cill Mac Nessan, pokes its head out of a field of bracken which in summer makes access almost impossible. This is all that remains of an important seat of learning, yet another that

reaches back to that ancient diaspora of Celtic saints and hermits fleeing from the temptations of life on the mainland. A monastic settlement was founded here by the three sons of Nessan, who was himself a prince of the royal House of Leinster. Like so many early saints the details of their lives are shadowy and confusing. Their names are given as Mó-Nessa, Diochuill, and Neslugh. They are said to have had four brothers, making a family of seven, all in the Church. But many early monks moved about from place to place so that several saints may have grown up around one individual. While the *Annals of the Four Masters* records how the Vikings were besieged on the island in 897 and plundered it in 960, they make no mention of the saintly brothers who may have lived around about the sixth century.

Everything about them is speculation. The little church has been dated to the seventh century, but even that date is conjectural.

The only historical evidence of Cill Mac Nessan relates to the Bull of Pope Alexander III in 1179, when it was mentioned as belonging to the See of Dublin. A half-century later, when hermetical traditions had become obsolete, what remained of the monastery was transferred to the mainland at the Abbey of St Mary's at Howth.

What seems beyond dispute is that monks in this rocky knob of land produced an outstanding work of Celtic scholarship. The copy of the four Gospels with two illuminated pages, known as the *Garland of Howth*, is believed to have been penned in ornate majuscule script some time in 690. Naturally, when the monks went from the island to Howth the sacred book went along as well.

If legend is to be believed this book of Gospels had a busy history. Few lives of Irish saints lack the interference of the Devil. The sons of Nessan were tempted by him, and to drive him away the book was hurled at him, falling into the sea. Years later, miraculously preserved except for its cover, it was caught in a net by an old fisherman.

Like the Golden Bell of Scattery and the Book Shrine of Molaise of Inishmurray, the Garland was used as a swearing rite for making oaths "so that even an innocent and religious man feared to be sworn on it." If guilty, the book would slip from his hands. Today the Garland of Howth can be seen in Trinity College, tangible evidence of the scholarship and love of God that saw to its creation on Ireland's Eye.

FAR LEFT: A yacht with sails furled slips past the stacks at the east end of the island.
ABOVE: Cormorants, one of the more familiar species of seabirds, are expert swimmers and divers.
LEFT: From Howth harbour a short boat ride lands the visitor at a sandy beach near the Martello Tower.

At one time Cill Mac Nessan possessed a small round tower rising from the chancel vault—one of nine similar churches once found in Ireland. The surviving ruin says little for nineteenth-century ideas of conservation, since the original west gable·was removed and shipped over to Howth to provide building material for the Catholic

unclear. Probably people from the mainland wished to be buried near the saints. The boatman who brought me over told me that there used to be buildings behind the strand, but these may have been summer houses.

It seems wrong that since 1852 Ireland's Eye is less known as the abode of the three saintly brothers than as "the rocky island

culties while swimming and he knew nothing about her fate, since he was painting at the time of her death. But they were the only people on the island, and he was not popular. He owed many of the locals money and in addition was guilty of adultery, a crime that many of his contemporaries thought as bad as murder. Arrested and charged, he was convicted

church. What was left of the original building was, in the opinion of later architectural pundits, "excessively restored." At the same time many human bones were dug up in what must have been an abandoned graveyard around the church. Whether they belonged to the early monks or inhabitants of the island is

where the wretched Kirwan murdered his wife" (in the words of a Victorian tourist). The story of how an outing turned to brutal tragedy swiftly became folklore. In 1852 a middle-class Dublin couple named Kirwan, on holiday at Howth, were rowed out to the island by boatmen in much the same way as tourists make their way out today. Kirwan, who was an amateur painter, set up his easel while his wife went off to bathe in the sea in order to relieve a skin ailment. She never returned and her body was found washed up at a place known as the "Long Hole."

Kirwan claimed that she had got into diffi-

on flimsy circumstantial evidence and sentenced to hang. He was reprieved to spend 27 years at hard labour before release. He is believed to have returned to the scene of his unfortunate wife's death before sailing for America to meet the "other woman."

Whatever the truth about the fate of Mrs Kirwan, the words of the brochure handed out to visitors sum up the atmosphere of Ireland's Eye: "Today the island is a pleasant peaceful place where one can relax and enjoy the wildlife and the beach and catch some fresh air and be oblivious to the happenings of the past."

ABOVE LEFT: A window in the oratory of Cill Mac Nessan, the Church of Nessan's Sons.
ABOVE RIGHT: Looking back across a sparkling summer sea towards Ireland and Howth harbour.
RIGHT: All that remains of the monastery founded by the three brothers in the sixth century.

THE SALTEES

Great Saltee, Little Saltee

THIS CHAIR IS ERECTED IN MEMORY OF
MY MOTHER, TO WHOM I MADE A VOW WHEN I
WAS TEN YEARS OLD THAT ONE DAY I WOULD
OWN THE SALTEE ISLANDS AND BECOME THE
FIRST PRINCE OF THE SALTEES
HENCEFORTH MY HEIR AND SUCCESSORS
CAN ONLY PROCLAIM THEMSELVES PRINCE
OF THESE ISLANDS BY SITTING IN THIS CHAIR
FULLY ROBED IN THE ROBES AND CROWN
OF THE ISLANDS AND TAKE THE OATH OF
SUCCESSION
MICHAEL THE FIRST

THE SALTEES

From the Star of the Sea Church overlooking Kilmore Quay the two Saltees, Great and Little, four kilometres (two-and-a-half miles) and six kilometres (three-and-a-quarter miles) away respectively are clearly visible. The Great Saltee is considerably bigger than its neighbour—88 hectares (219 acres) to the 39 hectares (98 acres) of the Little Saltee. The islands appear distant, but a curious submerged ridge created out of shingle known as St Patrick's Bridge connects the north-eastern point of the Little Saltee with the mainland beside Kilmore Quay.

The rocks that make up these islands are among the most ancient in Europe: Pre-Cambrian bedrock, at least six hundred million years old. Erosion has created jagged cliffs, caves, and strange rock formations, particularly on the south, east, and west sides, where congregate the great density of birds that make the Saltees famous.

There are no safe anchorages, and the raised beaches, created by glacial forces similar to those that formed St Patrick's Bridge, make landing on the islands difficult in disturbed weather. In winter storms and sea spray lash the rocks—perhaps giving the islands their name. But people have not been deterred from living in a place where the soil is rich, the fishing is abundant and there are copious birds' eggs in season.

The discovery of one ancient man-made flint proves the sojourn of Stone Age men over two thousand years before Christ. The presence of later Neolithic tribes is indicated by traces of dolmens, a promontory fort, ring forts, and circular huts discovered during an aerial survey of the Great Saltee in 1952.

An Ogham stone found here dates back to the early Christian era. But only a name—Abbey Field—together with faint traces of a rectangular building suggest that a Christian community once lived here. There is no Gaelic tradition or oral literature concerning the Saltees; instead the names of landmarks on the islands have an Anglo-Norman ring, perhaps deriving from the dialect of the people of Bargy on the mainland—Squire Hole, Frenchman's Well, Tailor's Well.

In Norman times the Saltees came into the possession of the monks of Tintern Abbey, England, and later, after the dissolution of the monasteries, were appropriated by the Colclough family. There followed a period when the islands were infamous as refuges for pirates, smugglers, and wreckers. Pirates included the seventeenth-century "Biscayners" from the Bay of Biscay, the

"Dunkirkers," and the "Algerines" from North Africa.

The islands were also a place of refuge. Fugitives like Captain Stafford, who commanded Wexford Castle when Cromwell sacked the town in 1649, hid on the Great Saltee. The two unfortunate leaders of the 1798 Rebellion, Beauchamp Bagenal Harvey and John Henry Coclough, sheltered in vain in a Saltee cave. They were betrayed and captured, and taken from there to their death in Wexford.

None of this recorded history suggests a settled community. However, in the nineteenth century the Great Saltee was colonised. Years ago I met a man named Andy Parle who told me how his ancestor, John Parle, had been shipwrecked off the Wexford coast and became part of a successful community which lived on the island for much of the nineteenth century.

The surrounding sea, which commands the approaches to the Bristol Channel and the trading ports of England, Wales, and Ireland, has been a graveyard for hundreds of vessels. Many laden with rich cargoes passed the south Wexford coast, notorious for shoals, reefs and rocks; other hazards included the breed of wreckers who would lead a ship to its doom with lanterns. More recently German submarines sank hundreds of ships in the sea area around the Saltees during both world wars.

The old Parle homestead on the north side of the island, now used by bird watchers, is surrounded by the ruins of other buildings, including one known as the School House. After the last Parle left the island in 1905 a succession of new occupants followed, the most recent being Michael Neale, the self-styled "Prince of the Saltees."

Today anyone landing on the Great Saltee is met with a notice proclaiming that he is trespassing on Princely soil:

"The Saltee Islands and the waters surrounding them are in absolute possession of the Prince of the Saltees and his heirs.

"No man or assembly of men has any right whatever to interfere in the affairs of the Saltee Islands."

But it is the birds which rule the Saltees—which have been described as "the most wonderful resort of birds in Great Britain or Ireland." They are extraordinary, not only for

on and around the Great Saltee…
a phenomenal concentration of breeding
sea birds is to be seen annually
during the summer months

their diversity but for their vast numbers. Of the 390 species on the Irish list, 223 can be found on the islands.

The low cliffs of the Little Saltee contain one of the most important sites in Ireland for breeding cormorants, while mallard, shelduck, and oystercatchers also breed on the Little Saltee. But it is on and around the Great Saltee that a phenomenal concentration of breeding sea birds is to be seen annually during the summer months. For many early spring migration takes place from March to May and they begin to depart by mid-August. But then there are few months when some sort of migration does not take place.

Visitors brought across from Kilmore Quay disembark (sometimes with difficulty) on the north shore and make their way past the Prince's monuments and a line of cordyline palms to the southern side, where an assortment of crags and caves provide ideal accommodation for nesting sea birds. The dedicated watcher will camp overnight to hear the raucous calls of shearwaters returning to their burrows from fishing trips which have carried them as far away as the Bay of Biscay. Puffins also live in burrows—their strong webbed feet are adapted for digging with claws to which little hooks are attached. They scrape out the sand to create nesting holes, and are best seen in the early morning, but there are nearly always some of their clown faces to be seen at other times of day.

A bird to offer similar delight is the gannet, Ireland's largest sea bird, identified by its black-tipped wings, tobacco-coloured head and staring pale blue eyes. In July the absurd Disney-esque fledglings, with their huge beaks and their baby down like lambs' wool, sit on the Makestone and Bird Rock while their screeching parents are thrown up in the sky like feathers. The thousands of birds that make up the gannetry on the Great Saltee have multiplied from two pairs which were observed nesting here in 1929.

Another favourite species must be the guillemots, which float in vast numbers off the rocks of the south side. Guillemots are the northern hemisphere's answer to the Antarctic penguin and, like the king penguin, their breeding habits are supremely uncomfortable. They prefer small open rock ledges where they huddle together in scores side by side. They make no nest, but lay a single egg on bare rock, often stuck to its precarious site with some guano. Eggs are pyriform or

ABOVE: Kittiwakes nest on the cliff face. Their name is an imitation of this small gull's cry.

pear-shaped so that they will not roll off easily, but even so, many fall over the edge onto the rocks below. They have different colours and patterned markings which vary enormously so that two eggs side by side, which may be green, blue, brown or reddish, look as if they belong to different species. It is believed that these variations allow birds to recognise their eggs in the crowd.

Razorbills, black-backed gulls, fulmars, and the night-haunting shearwaters are here in their thousands. The Great Saltee is the most easterly outpost in the south of Ireland for the chough. Inland, mallard, shelduck, and lapwing breed, together with some forty species of more common land birds. Counts of breeding birds vary—for example, an avian disease hit the guillemots in the 1970s so that the population dived, although it has made a recovery since then. The peregrines have gone and so have the swallows. Although increasing pollution and scarcity of fish concern many ornithologists, the numbers have not yet fallen to any worrying degree. It is estimated that around a hundred-and-fifty thousand birds congregate on the Saltees by the end of the breeding season and some species like the shearwaters and gannets are on the increase.

From the Saltees on a warm summer's day you can view the sweep from the Hook peninsula and its lighthouse to the Tuskar Rock; much of the coastline is banded by miles of strand, including Baginbun, where the Normans first landed in Ireland. In the distance beyond the green Wexford landscape the fairy mountain Slievenamon is visible, the line of the Comeraghs, and eastward the dome of Mount Leinster. Here on the Great Saltee man's loss of habitation has been nature's gain. Pirates, Norman monks, Stone Age man, smugglers, rebels, wrecks, Parles, and Prince Michael are all part of the history of these unique islands, but today the Saltees are strictly for the birds.

ABOVE: Gannets nest in two dense colonies along the southern shore. The adults are white all over, with the exception of black wing tips and a tobacco-coloured head. Each pair raises a solitary chick, covered with a white down like cotton wool.

GREAT ISLAND

GREAT ISLAND

PREVIOUS PAGE: Five
Martello Towers like this
one near Belvelly Castle
were built around the
approaches to Cork as
defences during the
Napoleonic Wars.
LEFT: The Italianate
veranda of the old Royal
Cork Yacht Club, which
evolved from the Water
Club, the world's first
yacht club, founded at
Haulbowline in 1720.
ABOVE: The town of
Cobh, dominated by St
Colman's cathedral, was
the main point of depar-
ture for Irish emigrants
to the United States.

In the mid-1950s I embarked on a ship's tender for the S.S. *America*, which lay anchored off the port of Cobh. An east wind was blowing and an occasional down-pour made the town and the spire of St Colman's cathedral vanish into murky gloom. I looked back at the view seen by thousands of emigrants departing Ireland for the New World—the town and its cathedral which spreads along the south side of Great Island. The liner waited with her blazing lights and luxurious interior, rich scents of food, uni-formed bell hops, and loud American voices greeting the windswept Irish passengers.

The S.S. *America* was one of 10,000 ships which have made a stop here over a period that covers more than two thousand years. Great Island and Cobh harbour with its fore-ground of Spike and Haulbowline islands have been linked to ships and shipping since before the birth of Christ, when Phoenician vessels called into the harbour to barter wine and silks for the wood of the oak trees that were being felled on the island. Around A.D.120 Ptolemy, the Greek geographer, gave Cork Harbour the name of "Dabrona." Subsequently, when it came under the control of the Celtic O'Lehanes, it was known as *Oileán Arde Crich*—Great Island— until the

Norman Barrys took it over and renamed it "Barrymore." Vikings, who found here an easy access to the rich lands of Munster, and other Normans like the Hodnetts, who built Belvelly Castle, all played their part in the island's history.

In 1666 the Earl of Orrery wrote how "were I an enemy and to invade Ireland, I would land in the Great Island of all places, for it stands in Cork harbour, has but one pass into it, and is above six miles about, a fertile place, and nothing to oppose their landing there, which also is in the midst of the best quarters, almost equally distant from Cork, Youghall, and Kingsale." However, the development of the town of Cobh (formerly spelt "Cove") as a port did not come for another century. Although convoys of merchantmen assembled in the harbour during the seventeenth cen-tury, as late as 1750 Cobh was described by Charles Smith as a village "mostly inhabited by seamen and revenue officers." But as the British navy developed, the strategic impor-tance of the area came to be recognised. Cobh faced onto its great harbour, huge and safe; five kilometres (three miles) long and three kilometres (two miles) broad, virtually land-locked, it was capable of sheltering the whole of the British navy.

Fleets assembled here for the American War of Independence and the subsequent war against France. During the nineteenth century the harbour was the assembly point for troopships sailing to the Crimea. Up until the First World War the power of the British navy would have been woefully restricted without the amenities of Queenstown and the naval base at Haulbowline Island, whose history includes a fort built by Lord Mountjoy against a threatened Spanish invasion. Until the emancipation of slaves in 1829 ships from Cobh participated in the slave trade, to the benefit of many Cork merchants.

On Spike Island, barely a kilometre (less than half a mile) from Cobh, the fort and garrison became the chief coastal defence for the south of Ireland. The British would insist on retaining Spike at the foundation of the Irish state for the use of its navy. Its return to Ireland in 1938 together with other Treaty ports gave Prime Minister de Valera the means to establish neutrality during the

Second World War and affected the course of Irish history.

An anonymous tourist wrote his impression of a summer's day in 1870 when "the channel fleet had arrived the day previous, and their noble forms, with the great number of smaller craft, gunboats, etc., and the numerous steamers constantly passing gave a most lively appearance....The blue water shone and sparkled...the monster ships stood like huge sentinels in a row, and the brisk little steamers puffed and whistled."

But at the same time that the navy made its presence felt, the town on Great Island was pre-eminently a place of departure, often in tragic circumstances. Before the building of the prison on Spike Island in the 1840s, convicts were assembled in the floating hulk *Surprise* in the harbour to await transportation, first to the West Indies, and later, throughout the first half of the nineteenth century, to Australia. An old ballad referred to their plight:

Tis there's the hulk that's well stored with convicts
Who were never upon decks till they went to sea;
They'll ne'er touch dry land, nor rocky island
Until they spy land at sweet Botany Bay.

The forest of masts floating in the harbour included those of hundreds of emigrant ships. Some—too many—deserved the name of coffin ships, as fever swept through their holds during the years following the famine. But over the decades the vast majority of emigrants made the journey safely, even in sailing ships that might be blown forwards for two days and backwards for three.

After sail turned to steam, emigrants continued to pour out of Ireland through Queenstown. In the early years of this century more than twenty thousand would leave from Queenstown each year. There were often up to five liners in the harbour at one time awaiting the arrival of passengers brought out in tenders like the *Flying Fish*, *Ireland* or *America*. Even in the 1920s and '30s there were few families in Munster without a relative who had "taken the boat."

In 1838 the little *Sirius*, the first steam-paddle ship to cross the Atlantic, set out from here, inaugurating "the age of steam." In 1861 the great Victorian engineer Brunel's *Great Eastern*, heralded as the finest development in ship architecture of its time, but notorious for its instability and its seasick passengers, was towed into the harbour, having been disabled by heavy seas. Other liners associated with Queenstown were less lucky. On April 10 1912 crowds of people made the excursion

LEFT: Belvelly Castle, on the northern approach to Great Island, was built in the fourteenth century.
ABOVE LEFT: Haulbowline Island seen from Cobh. Yachts have raced here for nearly three centuries.
ABOVE CENTRE: St Colman's cathedral, built in the French Gothic style, was begun in 1868.
ABOVE RIGHT: The monument by Jerome O'Connor commemorating the sinking of the *Lusitania*.

to Queenstown to view what they were told was the greatest ship ever built and watch passengers sailing out on the tender from the quay of the White Star Line to the doomed *Titanic*.

Meanwhile the town itself had prospered as a naval base and holiday destination for citizens of Cork. The Barry and Broderick families were instrumental in turning Cobh into a fashionable watering place and a health centre. A temporary name change took place after August 2, 1849, when Queen Victoria paid her state visit here. According to her diary: "to give the people the satisfaction of calling the place Queenstown, in honour of it being the first spot on which I set foot upon Irish ground, I stepped on shore amidst the roar of cannon, and the enthusiastic shouts of the people."

On the front stands the old building of the Royal Cork Yacht Club (now a tourist office), the oldest yacht club in these islands, owing its origin to the "Water Club of the Harbour of Cork," which was established in 1720.

Today Cobh has changed from a centre for shipping into an industrial outpost. In 1938

INSET, LEFT: The crest of the Cunard Steamship Company Ltd, in Cobh Museum.

INSET, RIGHT: Detail of the mosaic floor of the old Royal Cork Yacht Club showing the club crest.

Irish Steel established a base on Haulbowline; across the harbour you can see the chimneys of the oil refinery at Whitehaven. Behind, the massive cathedral of St Colman dominates the Victorian terraces and the cascading houses at West View, known as the "pack of cards" built for families of men serving in the old police barracks opposite.

St Colman's foundation stone was laid in 1868. The spire was only completed in 1915 and the famous carillon, the largest in Ireland, was installed in 1916. Roofed in 1879, when the first Mass was celebrated, the 47 years it took to complete covered the period of greatest mass emigration.

The elegant little station no longer brings trainloads of emigrants seeking a new life. Instead it has been turned into a heritage centre, a model of its kind.

Behind the town to the north stretch the rolling green fields and woods that make up most of Great Island—the fiefdom of the Barry family. A little way out of town is the old graveyard of Clonmel, whose Gaelic name, *Clunmeala*, means "the Meadow of the Wild Bee's Nest" or "the Vale of Honey." Here around the ninth-century church of St John the Baptist is a graveyard that has been

described as the most cosmopolitan in Ireland. British military and naval tombstones stand in lines. Together with drowned sailors a countess of Huntington is buried here, alongside a duellist, a surgeon from Cobh, James Verling, who attended Napoleon on St Helena, and Vice-Admiral Stokes, whose rank entitled him to an ostentatious tomb. Inside the roofless church is the tomb of the Rev. Charles Wolfe, who is famous for one poem, *The Burial of Sir John Moore* ("Not a drum was heard, not a funeral note ….").

The victims of the *Lusitania* also lie in Clonmel. On Friday May 7, 1915 after she sank off the Old Head of Kinsale, nearly twelve hundred bodies were brought into Queenstown and laid out in makeshift morgues. On the Monday, when the mass burials took place, for much of the day the sound of wheels of improvised hearses was heard in the streets. The Peace Memorial, begun by Jerome Connor and completed after his death by Donal Murphy, recalls the time when the town resembled a giant morgue. The processions of coffins, accompanied by escorts from the Connacht Rangers and the Royal Dublin Fusiliers, climbed up through the town to the three mass graves that awaited them there. In this quiet place the world surrounding Great Island has come together from the seven seas.

SHERKIN

SHERKIN

PREVIOUS PAGE: Sherkin "Abbey," in reality a friary, was founded in 1460 for Franciscans of the Strict Observance.

LEFT: Baltimore beacon on the mainland, known as Lot's Wife, is a landmark for boats making the crossing to Sherkin.

ABOVE: From Cow Strand, looking towards shrouded Cape Clear— belying its name.

In the 1960s the ferryman to Sherkin was John-Willie, one of those much loved characters for which West Cork is famous.

John-Willie was the Master, no boat could travel faster,
There never was disaster on the good old Dún an Óir ....

In fact the *Dún an Óir*, carrying passengers, mails, and general goods between Sherkin and Baltimore, rarely left on time— the constant rumour being that John-Willie was still in the pub. In those days before the deluge of tourism time seemed to matter less. Today the service is more punctual and John-Willie is no longer at the helm, but the approach across the short crossing has not changed as the boat leaves Baltimore for the brief chugging journey over a stretch of water, sheltered by the bay, whose entrance is marked by the white beacon known as Lot's Wife. After ten minutes or so the boat ties up at Abbey Strand, dominated by the grey tower of Sherkin Abbey.

Close by, almost falling into the water, the broken walls and fortifications of the castle of *Dún na Long*, the Fort of the Ships. This "goodly castle and bawn" is an O'Driscoll stronghold strategically built on an earlier promontory fort. Having moved to West Cork from Munster in the early Middle Ages, the powerful sept of the O'Driscolls shared with the O'Mahoney clan the control of the waters south of the Mizen which provided one of the richest fishing grounds off Europe. Fleets from France and Spain paid exorbitant dues to the O'Driscoll chieftains. In the fifteenth century the O'Driscolls demanded that "Every ship that fisheth…between the Fastnet Rock and the Staggs is to pay ten shillings and two pence, a barrel of salt, a hog's head of wine and a dish of fish three times a day."

Sherkin, being part of the O'Driscoll territory, not only benefited from these fishing tolls but also shared in the sept's turbulent history as its fortunes were bound up with those of Baltimore. Clan rivalry led to the raid of 1537 by Waterford men to punish the O'Driscolls for their involvement in the capture of four valuable cargo ships trading with Lisbon. Three ships landed their men on Sherkin, captured Dún na Long, burnt the Franciscan friary and 50 O'Driscoll pinnaces. They took away to Waterford as booty the great 30-oared galley of Fineen O'Driscoll before crossing the water to burn down the castle at Baltimore.

The Friary, generally and incorrectly known as "the Abbey" and situated just above the pier, was founded around 1460 by Fineen or Dermot O'Driscoll for the Franciscans. The three-storey sacristy and tower was built later, probably after the Friary's mauling by the Waterford men. Its most famous alumnus was the scholar Maurice O'Fehilly, who became a doctor of divinity at Padua University, wrote a dictionary of the Holy Scriptures and was known as Flos Mundi because of his learning.

The Friary continued to be used as a holy place after the Reformation. "I do bequeath my soul to Almighty God and my body to be buried in the Abbey of Sherkin," wrote a Richard Coppinger in his will of 1650. After it went into disuse Lionel Becher of Sherkin used the outside walls as a curing house for fish, and the holes that contained the press for

pilchards can still be seen. Meanwhile the people of Sherkin were obliged to use a Mass rock above Kinish harbour, which can still be seen.

Sherkin has its patron saint, St Mona, a female hermit who was born and lived here. There is a townland called Kilmona, derived from *Cill Mughaine*, the Church of St

Mona,"with traces of an ancient church and churchyard. A holy well in the valley west of Horseshoe harbour offers cures for the sick who make nine circuits and listen for the sound of bird song; if the invalid hears a bird singing within he will be cured.

Like other islands Sherkin became land-lord property. The Bechers, who took over from the O'Driscolls, were descendants of one of the Elizabethans who swept through Cork after the Desmond Rebellion at the end of the sixteenth century. They acquired vast tracts of West Cork, including Cape Clear and Mount Gabriel. On Sherkin a Becher first established himself in Dún na Long early in the seventeenth century, where as governor of the castle he was paid ten shillings a year. Later generations built a fort and then a house beside the castle; Bechers were living in Dún na Long in 1768, but castle and house have long since gone to ruin.

Like the O'Driscolls, the early Bechers depended on fishing for their income, in their case on the processing of pilchards that took place all around the coast of West Cork. The oil from these fish was used for many purposes, like oiling harness and cart wheels. In the seventeenth century, according to Bishop Pococke, the French came to Sherkin for the pilchard fisheries and "made great fortunes out of them." But pilchards are notoriously unpredictable and at some unknown date the great shoals deserted the waters of West Cork so that herring and sprats had to be caught instead. The last Becher here handed back the Abbey to the Board of Works in 1892.

In 1631 Sherkin figured in the sack of Baltimore when two Algerian ships under the command of a Dutch renegade stormed the port and captured 110 prisoners who were taken to North Africa as slaves. Two centuries later when Thomas Davis wrote a narrative poem about the incident ("O blessed God, the Algerine is Lord of Baltimore!") he included a not-too-flattering impression of Sherkin: "Old Inisherkin's crumbled face looks like a moulting bird." The coastline is indeed indented and there is variety on this green and fertile island, whose two harbours, Horseshoe Bay in the east and Kinish to the west, almost cut the island in two. On the north coast are rocky and sandy coves and two sandy beaches at the west end are generally empty. These destinations make an easy and pleasant walk, although the local residents keep a number of ancient untaxed cars.

A little lane way to the north from the crossroads beside the Friary passes the remains of Dún a Long en route to the abandoned settlement of the Dock, which once contained a thriving shipyard. Most of the shipwrights who lived in the cluster of cottages here belonged to the Minihane family, who came to Sherkin from the mainland near Ballydehob. The names of the vessels built there, not only fishing boats, but other coastal ships also capable of the long voyage to America, are still remembered: they include the *John Field*, the *John and Mary*, the hooker *Ellen*, the *Beauty of Munster*, and the *Margaret Hughes*, which during the famine carried a load of fleeing islanders across the Atlantic to Canada.

The main route from Abbey Strand crosses the length of the island to the south. There is a turn off to Horseshoe Bay, almost landlocked, a circle of blue sea with a narrow opening cut through the cliffs. On the townland to the east slate quarries flourished. They were established in the nineteenth century by the Bechers whose slates were "warranted not to gather moss, nor crack from heat or fire and to resist the strongest acids." On the far side facing Cape Clear is the lighthouse, erected in 1885. When I visited Sherkin in the 1970s I stayed in Miss Donovan's cottage at the highest point above the bay; from her back window she would watch the liners passing on their way to America and the giant oil tankers destined for Bantry Bay.

The main road, if such a pleasant rural lane can be described as such, leads past the small National School, the church, a turn-off for the Silver Strand and the new marine station, and eventually reaches the sea at the west end. Above the high green headlands the summit of the gentle slope of Sliabh Mór provides a view of Roaring Water Bay and islands such as the Skeams, Heir Island, and the Calf islands. After Cape Clear, Sherkin is the second biggest of Carbury's Hundred

ABOVE LEFT: The castle of Dún na Long was built by the O'Driscolls overlooking Sherkin Sound.
BELOW LEFT: A small stone carving inside the Friary.
RIGHT: A traditional hooker sails past the southern cliffs of Sherkin toward the quiet waters of Baltimore harbour.

ABOVE: Looking north over Kinish harbour.
RIGHT: North-east over Ordeen Point towards Baltimore.
BELOW: Michael (centre) with friends William, Rowan, and Kian, and their teacher, Cait O'Reilly, attend the Sherkin Island National School.

Isles. (I have never been able to count up to anything like a hundred). To the south-west, only divided by the narrow waters of the island of Cape Clear, is the dreaded Gascanane Sound, studded with rocks and booming with Atlantic rollers at the east end of Cape Clear. Those who made the passage through the Gascanane for the first time were expected to improvise a short poem, perhaps to distract them from sea-sickness.

The soil of Sherkin is rich with an exceptionally varied vegetation. A modern detailed botanical survey revealed that the island contains well over five hundred species of plants; no other equivalent area in Ireland can offer so many. In the recent past when farming flourished, a typical smallholding might consist of a herd of cows, a horse, some hens, and the usual assortment of cats, kittens and dogs. The island's two creameries each had

their shop which carried supplies from bacon to barbed wire. But as small farms gradually became unsustainable, it was the same story as elsewhere.

Twenty years ago the resident population had dwindled to about seventy people, most of whom were pensioners. However, there has been something of a turnaround on Sherkin and it has managed to survive, if not flourish. Thirty years later the population is around

ninety, not an earth-shattering increase, but enough maybe to put the prospect of extinction at bay. In 1983 Sherkin was given a new community hall, and the small national school, built in 1892, maintains about a dozen pupils. A signal of renewal perhaps is that the Friary is undergoing a careful restoration by the Board of Works.

Things are not the same, of course. The old society based on the farming and fishing community is almost extinct, and many of those who have taken over and restored the old farm houses are newcomers. Other houses

> *"Old Inisherkin's crumbled face*
> *looks like a moulting bird."*
>
> THOMAS DAVIS

belong to those who only come here for the summer holidays. The easy access to Baltimore and the relative proximity of Cork make Sherkin attractive for those wishing to live on an island without having the hardship of a cruel sea-crossing to contend with. But there are also a number of new houses built by local couples intending to raise their families here, and others who had left for the mainland or emigrated have returned. The people of Sherkin today, consisting half of indigenous islanders and half of "blow-ins," seem to blend happily.

In the 1970s I wrote how "the atmosphere of Sherkin seems idyllic, neighbour befriending neighbour, living without rancour or competition. The islanders' houses, set in sunlit fields facing the sparkling Atlantic, always have their doors open." It is good to report that the atmosphere at the turn of the new century seems to be much the same.

CAPE CLEAR

CAPE CLEAR

PREVIOUS PAGE: Beyond a prehistoric passage tomb a new wind charger on the summit of *Cnoc Caraintín*, Quarantine Hill, captures power from the fierce Atlantic winds.

LEFT: The Fastnet Rock was known to passing emigrants as the Teardrop of Ireland. The lighthouse is now bereft of keepers.

ABOVE: Ruins of the O'Driscoll castle, *Dún an Óir*, the Fort of Gold, stands on a promontory that has broken away from the landmass.

Cape Clear has much the same relationship to the islands of Roaring Water Bay as Clare Island does to the islands of Clew Bay. Its four-and-three-quarter-kilometre (three-mile) length marks the southern boundary of Roaring Water. To the east the treacherous waters of the Gascanane Sound separate the Cape from Sherkin; to the west is the open Atlantic and the Fastnet Rock. To the south Cape Clear looks out on the Atlantic; to the north the scattering of islands in Roaring Water Bay leads the eye towards Schull harbour. Looking towards the Cape from the mainland at Schull, you can see a new silhouetted landmark on the top of the highest point on the island, Quarantine Hill—the two great arms of an electric wind-charger slowly rotating against the sky. They are a portent of the new forces that will affect the lives of islanders. Nearby are two equally significant structures from an earlier age—the old lighthouse and the signal tower, both built during the early years of the nineteenth century.

The signal tower was erected on the island's highest point as part of a chain of lookouts after Wolfe Tone and the French fleet had passed this way to their failed landing in Bantry Bay in 1796. Fear of Frenchmen was also reflected in the *fir breuga*, the false men,

upright stones placed above the south-west cliffs of Clear which were painted—or possibly clothed in uniforms—in order to discourage invaders.

The old lighthouse was superseded by the lighthouse on Fastnet Rock, painstakingly built with material carried out from Crookhaven on the mainland. Recently automated, the deserted lighthouse on the Fastnet sends out the same long beam of light that was once the responsibility of the vanished keepers.

Millions of emigrants who passed this way looked out at the hump of Cape Clear, the last they would see of their native land. On the island itself fires would be lit by relatives and friends for their departing kin to see, a dying beacon of love and hope. For passengers on the *Titanic* the Cape was their final landfall.

The island is almost cut in two by the south and north harbours, Ineer and Trawkieran. From the sea the north harbour, closed in on one side by cliffs, is almost completely hidden from view. Boats slide into it through a narrow inlet to the quays built by the Congested Districts Board at the turn of the nineteenth century. When I first visited the Cape in the 1960s I heard a ballad that reflected on the old days of mackerel and herring fishing:

The harbour of Trawkieran,
I saw it in its pride
With its fleet of yacht-like fishing boats
Awaiting for the tide.

Nowadays, during the summer, the harbour is always bustling as sailing boats make their way through the passage, and the ferry, *Naomh Ciaran II*, named after the island's saint, brings hundreds of students from all over Ireland. The population almost doubles largely because of the presence of two Irish colleges.

You need good legs to circumvent the many steep little roads, including the almost perpendicular rise of Locavuat, and inspect the little lake of Errul with its special cleaning qualities supposedly the result of some particularly active bacteria.

West of the north harbour on the edge of the cliff the ruins of the O'Driscoll castle of *Dún an Óir*, the Fort of Gold, are perched on the remains of a promontory fort. The castle was dismantled in 1601 after the Battle of Kinsale by the guns of Captain Roger Harvey,

who placed these on the high ground above it. Chunks of masonry dislodged by cannon and storm still lie among the rocks. Stories of treasure linger on and from time to time scuba divers can be spotted below the northern cliffs in search of coin and bullion. Perhaps they have heard how a ghost ship arrives at Dún an Óir at night and unloads a cargo of treasure. The castle is also associated with tales of Cape Clear's giant, Cruthair Ó Carevaun, who was nearly two-and-a-half metres (over eight feet) tall and died in the castle as a hermit.

In the last century Cape Clear's position as first landfall for ships calling from America gave it considerable significance as a stepping stone in communications. Before the development of the cable on Valentia, there was a transatlantic station at the south harbour. Steamers were met by the boatmen of Clear; dispatches and cables wrapped in waterproof cases were thrown overboard in floating containers and carried back to the mainland via Sherkin island for rapid transmission to London. News of the progress of the

American Civil War and the assassination of President Abraham Lincoln reached Europe in this way.

Traces of Neolithic and Bronze Age man include a "marriage stone," a gallaun penetrated by a hole; lovers have long linked hands through it, pledging fidelity. The axis of the hole points to the spot on the horizon where the sun rises at the summer solstice. Recently a prehistoric tomb was discovered on the island's highest point.

At the north harbour a pillar stone is inscribed with crosses on the front, the back, and the top, said to be etched by the hand of St Ciaran himself. Ciaran may have been the first Irish saint; certainly he was one of the earliest and seems to have preceded Patrick. He was born here in A.D.352, and it may be that the first Mass ever held in Ireland was celebrated on the island. His feast day, on the

ABOVE LEFT: The Fastnet Rock, seen in the distance, is the most southerly point in Ireland.
ABOVE RIGHT: Lovers link hands through the hole in this standing stone and pledge fidelity to one another.

5th of March, is celebrated by a blessing of the local boats, including the mail boat from Baltimore, with water from the holy well, which lies near the pillar stone. The ruins of a small Romanesque church are built on an earlier monastery founded by the saint. The Gaelic name of the island, *Inis Cléire*, means Island of the Clergy.

Most of Ciaran's life is a mystery. A dictionary of saints warns that most of what is related about the saint "however entertaining or edifying, has no value in sober history."

One story tells of an incident during his boyhood when he saw a hawk swoop down and snatch a fledgling from his nest. The young Ciaran prayed for the little bird, whereupon the hawk flew down and laid it, torn and bleeding, at his feet; another prayer resulted in it being made whole again. This anecdote is appropriate because in all Ireland there is no better place for birds than Ciaran's birthplace of Cape Clear. The Saltees have their great colonies of nesting sea birds, but Clear has a particular avian distinction. The island's geographical position results in hundreds of thousands of birds of passage passing beneath its cliffs during the significant months of migration.

Nearly three hundred out of the 400 species found in Ireland have been recorded here since the Bird Observatory on the north harbour was established in 1959. Out beyond the southern headlands and the cliffs at Blanarragaun up to thirty thousand Manx

shearwaters an hour pass in late July and August. Other sea birds include fulmars, gannets, Arctic skuas, great skuas, kittiwakes, razor bills, and guillemots.

In October the twitchers are to be seen, gathered in flocks, easily identifiable by their binoculars and cameras. Their patience has been rewarded with the sighting of many rarities, such as Cetti's warbler, Montagu's harrier, the olive-backed pipit, the Siberian thrush, as well as the Pallas grasshopper warbler from the east.

Other visitors can witness the arrival every second year of the yachts of the Fastnet Race tacking up along the south coast from Cowes if the wind is in the west; the turn around the Fastnet Rock and the sudden billowing of their spinnakers is as fine a sight as a few thousand shearwaters.

One of the island's best-known inhabitants was Conchur Ó Sióchain, born on the Cape in 1866, who came to be known as "The Man from Cape Clear" after his memoirs were published in 1940. He observed how on the mainland at Baltimore, nine kilometres (less than six miles) away: "I hear that scarcely a word of Irish is being spoken in that place." He went on: "The same thing all but happened among ourselves. What I would compare our situation to is just as if a fire would be out except that a few burning embers still remained in the ashes of the fireplace. That is the way it is with Irish."

Ó Sióchain, who lived all his life on the island, never dreamed for a moment that the Cape would be deserted the way the Blaskets and so many other islands would be. There is every hope that he is right, and the Cape Gaeltacht lives on.

TOP: Cattle from Clear are brought ashore at Baltimore harbour from the island ferry.

RIGHT: Looking across the northern shore at Cnocán na mBairneach.

DURSEY

DURSEY

Dursey is so close to the mainland in West Cork that a strong arm could throw a stone across the dividing channel which is 200 metres (220 yards) wide at its narrowest point. But Dursey Sound, which divides the island from the Beara peninsula, has always been a fearful place for boatmen and seamen alike. High winds and storms have contributed to Dursey's isolation, which was as extreme as that of other islands much further from Ireland's shore.

For this reason, in the early twentieth century, the old harsh ways that just a couple of hundred yards over the water had become a thing of the past, were preserved on the island. Over the years the people of Dursey developed into a gruff, idiosyncratic community, self-reliant, difficult to approach and having little time for those who did not share their hardships.

In 1969 when I first visited the island, all this was set to change. There were plans to link the island with the mainland by means of a cable car with the capacity of taking six passengers or one large cow with attendant.

For many years a bridge had been talked about but nothing had happened. Now, due to the efforts of Father Matthew Keane, the contract for assembling the cable car had been given to a Scottish company. Two giant metal pylons on either side of the channel would carry the cable 22 metres (75 feet) over the high-water level, allowing room for ships to pass underneath. Passengers would be conveyed by a hand-operated winching gear, and in case the mechanism broke down, a klaxon was being installed which would hoot to attract attention as the car swung helplessly over the water. Although the plans for the enterprise put cheapness as a priority, soon it was understood that pulling ropes by hand in order to get the thing going would be too hard a task for the old people. The winch was made mechanical.

On a rainy day in December 1969 the Taoiseach (Prime Minister) at the time, Jack Lynch, cut a ribbon across the door of the new cable car, and he and Mrs Mairead Lynch and four local worthies entered it and crossed the sound. I have always admired the pioneering bravery of these people, since on subsequent visits I have found the cable car a daunting method of progression. It is like crossing in a cupboard. However, since its inauguration the service has continued to carry across the people of Dursey together with their cattle, sheep and donkeys. Among the various celebrities who have made the intimidating crossing are Mary Robinson, Bishop Eamonn Casey, and the novelist Jilly Cooper.

The island measures six-and-a-half by two-and-a-half kilometres (four by one-and-a-half miles) across, but the steep cliffs and the three great hills give a feeling of bulk. The three tiny villages seem correspondingly minute, their houses built of blocks of stone with windows tunnelled through the walls as thick as the length of a man's arm.

On my first trip to Dursey I camped near the broken walls of St Mary's Abbey, whose graveyard contains the large stepped vault of the family of O'Sullivan Beare. A short distance away is the jutting headland of Oileán Beag on which there are the outline remains of a small fort built by Diarmuid O'Sullivan in the late sixteenth century to control the sound. Once the castle had a drawbridge linking it to the island proper. "A place of exceeding great strength," it was the scene of one of the most violent episodes of the Elizabethan wars.

A description of what happened to the castle and its defenders comes from the seventeenth-century historian Philip O'Sullivan, who was born on the island around 1592. Much of what we know about Dursey's past comes from his pen. He describes "a small island…which is very strongly seated by nature, by reason of the difficulty of landing, which is convenient but in one narrow entrance which may be defended by a few hands; and besides it is impossible for any boat to arrive at this entrance except it be dead calm, the least gale of wind raising such billows as to endanger any boat that should come near the shore."

In June 1602 the island was crowded with refugees from Sir Peter Carew's invasion, together with a garrison to defend the castle. Tragically the thirteenth day of June was calm, enabling a large English force to cross the sound. In Philip O'Sullivan's words: "The garrison was put to the sword. Some ran their swords up to the hilt through the babe and mother who was carrying it to her breast, others paraded before their comrades little

BELOW: Encouraging a cow to fly. One at a time is the maximum load.

children writhing and convulsed upon their spears, and finally, binding all the survivors, they threw them into the sea over jagged and sharp rocks, showering on them shots and stones. In this way perished three hundred Catholics." The area where the cable passengers land is called *Áit an Fheoir*, the Place of the Massacre.

The island's ancient sites, many of which have only been investigated in recent years, range from a standing stone, a holy well, and ancient hut sites to the two churches. The ruin of Kilmichael Church stands on an earlier foundation built by the monks of Skellig Michael.

You can walk the final few miles of what is called the Beara Way through the three dwindling townships and their scattered groups of houses. Beyond Kilmichael is the Needle's Eye, a narrow passage between a cliff once passed by Dursey women in the belief that afterwards they would never die in childbirth. Above on Tilickafinna is a signal tower, one of those built during the Napoleonic Wars as a

look-out for possible invading French ships; a code known as the flag-and-ball system flown from the flagstaff linked the tower with another within sight on Black Ball Head and from there was relayed to other towers around the coast.

At the final precipitous outcrop of Dursey Head the view is stupendous. From the bare slopes of the hill the horizon stretches ahead to America; on the land side are the three peninsulas of Sheep's Head, Three Castle Head, and the far off Mizen dug into the ocean like the prongs of a fork. Beyond are the rolling blue mountains of Kerry and Cork. Once again where human life has ebbed wildlife has taken over, and the island has been designated as a Natural Heritage Area for wildlife conservation. To the north-west, the Bull with its lighthouse, and the Cow

Rock, line up along the entrance to the Kenmare river. The Calf Rock lies to the south-west. Both the Bull Rock, which contains the largest gannetry in Ireland, and the Cow, have come under a Special Protection Act for Wild Birds.

It may be the cruel past that gives Dursey its air of melancholy, or merely the feeling that the cable car came too late. In 1969, although there was a small functioning school, soon to close, and even a telephone, there was no electricity or running water, no pub or church. The only way of getting cattle to market was to swim them across the Sound. More and more people were leaving each year. Three-quarters of the houses were empty, their windows boarded up, the pathways to the doors blocked with nettles. I remember how the post office had run out of cigarettes, and all that was offered for sale was matches. Nothing else, certainly no drink.

Today Dursey has electricity and you see the occasional car and tractor. Some of the old houses have been done up by outsiders. But most are still empty. It is unsurprising that the number of permanent inhabitants is down to single figures. For the most part the island's bleak beauty is for the enjoyment of strangers who have swung easily in the metal gondola over the treacherous Sound.

THE SKELLIGS

THE SKELLIGS

Glib descriptions soon run out of adjectives to convey the spectacle of the two great pyramids composed of sandstone and slate veined with quartz west of Bolus Head, on the coast of south-west Kerry. Millions of years ago the peaks of submerged mountains were subjected to severe frosts, which expanded in the joints and faults of the rock and prized it apart. On a clear day they emerge like cathedral spires, or "like two hands raised in prayer."

In late May the Lesser Skellig has its rocky crevices salted white with nesting birds on every ledge. Twenty thousand or so pairs of gannets have made their breeding base here and created the largest gannetry in the world.

The birds that crowd on the 18 hectares (44 acres) of the largest island, Skellig Michael, include fulmars and Manx shearwaters, who rest by day in burrows from where you occasionally hear their rattling cry. But it is not for these, nor the kittiwakes, razor bills, or the odd puffin that you make the long journey over heaving water. Birds take second place to the true miracle of the island dedicated to the saint of high places.

On this isolated rock, consisting of sharply angled twin peaks 214 and 195 metres (715 and 650 feet) above the sea, a group of monks, following the lead of the Desert Fathers, made their home in A.D.600. The settlement was supposedly founded by one St Fionan, who was squint-eyed. There may have been a second St Fionan who was a leper; or perhaps St Fionan was both leprous and squinted—the Annals are not clear. The aspiring anchorites rowed out 12 kilometres (eight miles) in slender, hide-covered currachs.

Strong swells and currents meant that there were many days when it was impossible to land or embark. But the monks persisted, and here at the limit of the known world St Fionan's disciples and their successors endured harshness and isolation in the name of God.

In spite of a millennium of storms, Skellig Michael remains the most perfectly preserved of ancient monastic sites. The monks carried up stone and constructed their huts on the more sheltered east side, away from the prevailing wind, overlooking a precipice that falls 165-180 metres (550-600 feet) to the pounding waves in a position that has been described as being "built virtually on air." Their situation makes them the most dramatic structures in Western Europe, and can be compared with monasteries in the

Himalayas perched on precipices on snow mountains.

Steps hewn out of the rock made the high places accessible. Half-way to the two summits is a cross carved out of the rock. At Christ's Saddle are two stone crosses and terracing; to the west is South Peak with a rock-chimney known as Needle's Eye, and near the peak a remote ruined oratory.

The monastery itself is approached from Christ's Saddle by a steep flight of steps to the north-east. The six corbelled beehive clochans and a boat-shaped oratory similar to that at Gallarus are contained in two protective enclosures, together with a later church known as St Michael's Church. The cemetery contains twenty-two early gravestones. In addition, to the north east there is a second smaller oratory outside the enclosures.

The monks were supplied with water by five storage wells collecting channelled rain water, which still function. For fuel they must have used the roots of the sea pink which burns like poor quality turf; but turf must also have been ferried out from the mainland. Their diet has been largely deduced as being similar to that of the monks on the excavated site at Church Island near Valentia. Crops such as peas, beans, and onions would have been planted in the minute rock-girt garden on soil and seaweed laboriously collected from rock crevices. Like the lighthouse keepers after them, they probably grazed sheep and goats, while there was plenty of protein nearby in the form of birds and their eggs. Fish and shellfish would have also formed a major part of their diet. Probably they were able to catch the occasional seal, like those which can still be seen in the water waiting to snap up tired or sick birds at high tide.

The Annals confirm that the monks' aus-

tere calling was interrupted violently by the Vikings in A.D.823. In spite of its impregnable appearance, "Skellig was plundered by the heathen and Etgal was carried off into captivity and he died of hunger and thirst." After 1044 there is no historical mention of the monks of Skellig Michael.

In the face of winter storms and unrecorded hardships this extreme form of monastic discipline lasted until the twelfth century. Even at that time a new church was built of stone ferried with imaginable difficulty across from Valentia. But that may have been for the benefit of pilgrims, since the rule that demanded such rigorous self-denial was gradually yielding to more unified diocesan organisation. The community on Skellig

Michael resisted the new order. For a time they refused to accept a new date for Easter, so that marriages could be celebrated on the island on dates when they were prohibited on the mainland. But eventually the monks succumbed to change and the clochans were abandoned as they joined the mainland Augustinian house at Ballinskelligs.

Skellig Michael took on a new role as a place of pilgrimage. Up until the nineteenth century pilgrims rowed out and clambered around the various penitential stations. A guidebook for 1878 repeats some of the pilgrim's difficulties: "The penance consists in passing, or rather squeezing, first through a circular aperture in the rock … called 'The Needle's Eye,' and then by creeping up the smooth surface of a sloping stone to reach a little platform about 1 yard in width, the sides of which slope down to the ocean below … The ascent is so difficult and frightful that it is called 'The Stone of Pain.'"

Today's visitors to Skellig Michael are less masochistic. On a fine summer's day, perhaps after visiting the Skellig Heritage Centre on Valentia Island, tourists join the small armada of boats that sets off from Portmagee on the mainland. The journey takes around one-and-a-half hours.

On the day that I disembarked patience was needed as a fleet of boats, each containing up to a dozen people, had to wait its turn before approaching the difficult landing place on the south side at Cross Cove. On that summer's day I counted 100 tourists.

The crowds slowly climbed the tiers of steps leading to the hermitage; an all-round figure of 2300 steps has been given, each step a proof of religious zeal and dedication. From

ABOVE: The corbelled dry-stone cells constructed by the monks of Skellig Michael are perfectly preserved.

Christ's Saddle a final ascent of 600 leads to the monastery. At this high point of summer there was a certain amount of congestion on the narrow trail as the line of figures moving up and down recording the scene with cameras and camcorders. But the sense of awe and amazement overcame impatience. Who were the anchorites and holy men who built this wonderful place hanging on the edge of space?

Like so many other islands off Ireland, even the Skelligs fell into the hands of landlords, and the Butler family of Waterville paid a token rent to the English Crown of "two hawks and a quantity of puffin feathers yearly."

In 1820 the rocks were bought by the public body which became the Commissioners of Irish Lights, and by 1826 a lighthouse began operation. A considerable achievement (if not quite comparable to the buildings erected by the monks), it was badly needed. Scores of ships had come to grief on the Skellig rocks, among them the *Lady Nelson* sailing from Oporto to London. "The mate had warned the captain during the evening of his proximity to this dangerous rock; but the captain, who was drunken and jealous (his wife seconded the representations of the mate) put the vessel

> *The monastery is one of the wonders of the world—it is up there with the Taj Mahal, or Mount Everest.*

about and she struck."

Life was not easy for the succession of lighthouse keepers. Hugh Redmond lost both his sons and nephew over the cliffs, while another man fell to his death while cutting hay for his cow. In the ruin of the medieval church among the ancient graves of the monks is the poignant gravestone erected to the sons of another keeper. It reads: Patrick and William Callaghan died on the island in 1868 and 1869 aged 2 years 9 months and 4 years 9 months.

Among the sterling achievements of Skellig lighthouse keepers was the saving of 51 seamen wrecked from the S.S. *Marina* in November 1916. Not only did they witness shipwrecks but also plane crashes. On two occasions during the Second World War a German and an American plane crashed into the sea around Skellig Michael.

With the disappearance of the keepers in 1987 when the lighthouse became automatic, the old isolation has returned, except for the few short months in summer when the islands are generously displayed to the world. At other times they vanish into mist and winter storms and there is nothing but the cry of birds and the heaving waters of the Atlantic.

What is the future of the Skelligs? Are they in danger of becoming a theme park? Perversely the tourists are less of a threat than the rabbit. Rabbit burrows, which are also used by shearwaters, have been there for a thousand years, but increasingly they threaten to undermine walls, while the sea pinks and wild campion diminish. The Board of Works, which takes admirable care of Skellig, is putting its mind to this problem. Meanwhile the monastery is one of the wonders of the world—it is up there with the Taj Mahal, or Mount Everest. It remains a privilege to climb up to the little group of beehive huts and the oratory and to imagine the lives of the monks. T. J. Westropp, who came here in 1905, brooded: "it seems so very lonely, so very far from that quiet world whose blue, grey and purpose headlands bound the Eastern view, that it takes little stretch of the imagination to see what a refuge such a place must have been to ardent self-conscious men fleeing from the temptations of great cities and decaying civilisations of the old world."

VALENTIA

VALENTIA

Valentia, which lies off the Ring of Kerry a little way from Cahirciveen, is 11 kilometres (seven miles) long by nearly five kilometres (three miles) wide; three mountains form a spine along its length the highest being Geokaun at 266 metres (888 feet). To the east, where it faces the mainland, fields stretch down to the sea; to the west the cliffs of Bray Head rise 240 metres (nearly eight hundred feet) in height, in "savage grandeur" according to a Victorian observer. From Bray Head, Alfred Lord Tennyson looked out on the length of the Dingle Peninsula, Dursey Head, the Bull, the Cow and the Calf rocks, as well as the pinnacles of the Skelligs and was inspired to write: "Break, Break, Break, on thy cold grey stones, O Sea."

Like Achill, Valentia is no longer a true island since the day in 1970 when the new bridge linked it to the mainland atPortmagee.

Before the loss of their old isolation, the inhabitants, separated from the rest of Kerry by a short ferry ride, indulged in the common island mentality of thinking themselves a separate state. They have always been proud of being a hardy race; an early description of life on Valentia refers to "men strong and healthful at four score or a hundred years in so much that some will jocosely assert that the sons are forced to bring out their old parents on the continent (as I may call it) of Ireland to die."

Until the beginning of the nineteenth century the "hardy race" made a meagre living out of farming and fishing. Then their home became famous for two reasons—slates and the Cable. By the standards of other places in the west of Ireland, nineteenth-century Valentia, with its quarry, which had kept men employed during the famine, and the flurry of activity generated by the laying and maintaining of the Atlantic cable, became relatively prosperous.

In those days Valentia was owned by land-lords—Trinity College, Dublin, and the Knights of Kerry. It was through the influence of successive Knights of Kerry that an area of the wild island was turned into a Victorian landlord's village and given the doll-like name of Knightstown.

In this remote corner of Kerry it is still startling to come upon a small town laid out as a landlord's village with the facilities of a substantial English seaside resort. Knightstown used to be described as "an out-post of Empire" perhaps unfairly. It was said that you could draw a line separating the communities who lived around Chapeltown

Geokaun slates revealed a sensational secret. On a stretch of old sandstone shoreline near Knightstown were discovered a series of footprints—150 in all—of one of the oldest amphibian dinosaurs in Europe. Unfortunately, these are at risk from thieves and vandals.

At the Chapeltown end many of those who lived "back the island" continued their hard traditional lives as fishermen-farmers. Islanders were famous for their skill and endurance in fishing for mackerel in open boats with seine nets.

Seine boats were open, carvel-built wooden boats approximately ten metres (thirty-three feet) long and nearly two metres (six foot six) wide on the beam. Each carried a crew of thirteen or fourteen, six or seven heavy oars and the heavy seine net itself.

Up until 1930 huge quantities of mackerel were caught, gutted by brawny young women known as "splitters," washed and salted in barrels. Most of these barrels of pickled mackerel were sent to the United States. Then at the end of the 1920s catches diminished ("the fish went away") and the American government imposed a tariff on all imported fish. The industry declined, and by the 1940s it was over.

In the 1850s the island, whose inhabitants made up the most westerly community in Europe, was selected as the terminal for the Atlantic Telegraph. Efforts to link the United States with Europe had lasted almost a decade. The first attempt failed and the cable parted in August 1957, after 600 kilometres (380 miles) had been laid by the *Niagara*, an American warship. In 1858 the cable successfully crossed the Atlantic to Newfoundland. It "spoke" at intervals during the next two

and Bray Head and those connected with Knightstown's miniature Victorian enterprise. On one side you smelt turf, on the other, coal. At one end Gaelic was spoken; at the other, the King's English. The difference was reflected in the two names of the island. The Spanish sounding Valentia was a corruption by strangers of the name of the adjacent sound, Béal Inse, while the old name was *Oileán Dairbhre*, the Island of the Oak Forest. Throughout the nineteenth century, island people continued to call their home "Dairery."

In 1816 the slate quarry at Geokaun above Chapeltown was opened and an internationally famous industry established. Old red sandstone slates from Valentia graced the roof of the British House of Commons, London, while the Public Record Office had 40 kilometres (25 miles) of its shelves constructed from slate to support its burden of paper. Slate was in demand for fish slabs, water-tanks, and dairy shelving. Slate from Geokaun was used for the paving of numerous railway stations, and sent as far away as Bahia in Brazil for use on the San Salvador Railway. Blocks sometimes up to nine metres (30 feet) long were quarried in long cave-like galleries before

being taken down, first in horse-drawn carts, later by a small railway, from the quarry to the Slate Yard at Knightstown. The Duke of Wellington's slate billiard table at Stratford Saye, enamelled so that it looked like marble, so impressed Prince Albert that he ordered one of his own for the use of the royal family at its country house at Osborne, situated on the Isle of Wight.

The quarry provided employment until a decline set in during the 1870s in the face of competition from Welsh slates. In the hard years that followed it was kept open briefly by the Knight of Kerry when the miners were paid in yellow meal. But the mine's eventual closure in 1884 led to wholesale emigration.

Recently the sandstone that formed

ABOVE LEFT: Archaeological excavation has uncovered these buildings at Bray Head.
BELOW LEFT: Downtown Knightstown was once described as "an outpost of Empire."

months but fell silent on October 20, 1858. Not until 1866, after another, stronger cable had been manufactured, was the Internet of the nineteenth century success-fully laid and Europe and America linked.

The Cable Station was situated in Knightstown, and the little town seethed with clerks, hotel keepers, coastguards, and the Station's employees. The majority of newcomers were English or Welshmen who had experience in the running of mines, and because of Valentia's perceived remoteness, many officials were given hardship allowances. Life was pleasant enough for this well-paid elite, with regular money coming in and a round of social and sporting engagements. After the visit of Prince Arthur of Connaught in 1869, Mrs Young's Hotel where he stayed was given the title "Royal." The Church of Ireland church, completed in 1885, accommodated a thriving congregation headed by the Knight of Kerry. In addition to the lifeboat station and hospital there was even a Mason's Hall.

Since the men who operated the cable transmitters were nearly all English, they were not enthusiastic about relaying the news of the Easter Rising of 1916, although one cable message did get through to the USA. But it was said that in spite of the differences of background and religion there was little friction between the communities.

The Knight of Kerry, we are told by *Murray's Handbook of Ireland* for 1878, lived "firmly seated in the affections of his tenants." He and his family resided at his seat at Glanleam, "prettily situated on a cliff overlooking the harbour."

The branch of the Norman Fitzgeralds connected with Valentia took the name for its head as The Knight of Kerry after the Battle of Callan in 1261. By the nineteenth century they had long been Anglicised. The two knights who directed much of the fortunes of Valentia during the nineteenth century were

TOP: Fossil footprints of a small early amphibian, a tetrapod, the second oldest so far discovered.
ABOVE: A grotto to Our Lady was created in the Marian Year 1954 at the entrance to Geokaun quarry.

Peter Fitzgerald, the nineteenth Knight, created a baronet, and his son Sir Maurice Fitzgerald, the twentieth Knight, intimate of royal circles, who because of his marriage to an heiress could live in considerable luxury at Glanleam. In 1901 Glanleam had an indoor staff of 14, game keepers, an outdoor staff averaging 30, and hot houses filled with peaches and nectarines. The nineteenth Knight, an enthusiastic gardener, organised the planting of rare South American shrubs. Long neglected, today the garden is gradually being restored to something of its old glory.

In 1913 the estate, together with the land owned by Trinity College, was taken over by the Congested Districts Board and the luxurious routine at Glanleam ceased. Much of the house was demolished after the family moved to England.

The Cable Station closed in 1965, while the meteorological station, which keeps the name of Valentia alive in every shipping forecast on these islands, now operates from Cahirciveen on the mainland. However, one great Victorian institution continues its work on the island; every year the lifeboat station, founded in 1865, adds to its proud record of saving life at sea. Volunteers for the lifeboat, all unpaid, are guided by the Marine Radio Station, which also calls out, if necessary, the Sikorski helicopter based at Shannon.

Today 600 people live on Valentia, a decline from the 1000 who lived there in the 1940s. They are largely sustained by the new industry, tourism. The Skellig Heritage Centre at the bridge facing Portmagee is one of the best of its kind. The slate quarry has been turned into an amenity area augmented by a touch of holiness—a tunnel from which slate was extracted has been converted into a Lourdes' grotto. Knightstown, with a tranquil air, is a gentle ghost town; the sedate terraces and substantial buildings united by the charming clock tower have shaken off the bustling echoes of a lost Victorian past.

BEGINISH

BEGINISH

Beginish, the name a variant of *Inishbeg* or Little Island, is a beautiful deserted island of 98 hectares (243 acres) lying beyond Knightstown and acting as a breakwater to Valentia Island.

On the north face a line of dark basaltic rocks, columnar like those of the Giant's Causeway, runs down to the sea. The bulk of Valentia protects it on the south and southwest sides, while more shelter is provided to the north and north-east by the mountain ridge that ends at Doulus Head. At the west end where the island is exposed to the Atlantic Ocean a spine of rocks divides two areas of extensive bog. Above, the summit of a little hill contains a ruined watch tower. At the east end, nearest to Valentia, another rocky spur cuts a golden strand in two.

Beginish and a tiny islet known as Church Island were inhabited in the Middle Ages. The evidence of man's presence in medieval times was untouched until a series of archaeological excavations in the 1950s revealed details of the lifestyle of a fishing community and a religious community dating back a thousand years.

On the promontory facing Church Island, a jumble of jagged rocks partly covered with sand had accumulated over the centuries concealing a number of structures over which grew grass. This grass cover was broken up by collapsing rabbit burrows. Slowly the sand and loose material was being blown away, revealing traces of human habitation.

By 1947 the foundations of two circular stone huts with jagged ruinous walls could be traced. The wind continued its work until, almost a decade later, traces of circular buildings were revealed, assumed to be houses. There were eight altogether, dispersed among small irregular fields marked out by stone walls. Crude animal shelters were identified, some of them semicircular structures facing the prevailing west wind. There were also a number of small cairns, indicating that some attempt had been made to clear the fields for arable purposes. Clinkers and a spread of charcoal and burnt stones near one of the houses indicated that some iron smelting had taken place.

When Professor O'Kelly, who led the excavation in 1954, tackled one of the stone-walled houses, half buried in sand, he uncovered a yurt-shaped hut, presumed to have been roofed with wooden beams and thatch. It had been built half-underground in order to shelter it from the fierce prevailing wind. Its walls were over three metres (11 feet) high

"LIR . RISTI . STIN . ThINA + [MUNUIKL]. RISTI. [RUN]. –

Lir Erected This Stone + M... Carved the Runes"

inside and one-and-a-half metres (five feet) high above ground level outside. In a treeless area the wood would have had to be brought here from some distance. Since wood was scarce material, the beams seem to have been carefully removed at the time that the hut was dismantled and the inhabitants left.

There were two rooms, one a small addition making a crude annex tacked onto one side. Inside the main room a generous hearth was found in the centre. This was much needed, since the underground floor, resting on boulder clay, was constantly wet as rain water from the roof came relentlessly inside. Small stones had been laid on the floor in an attempt to get away from the wet and midden material may have helped to absorb it. The room was filled to a depth of 45 centimetres (18 inches) with shells, mixed with stones and animal and fish bones. Outside the hut were additional piles of midden debris.

The people in this household ate ox, pig, and sheep. Net and line sinkers were found which had been used to obtain the fish. Quantities of bones were found, principally of the ballan wrasse, which is still found in the waters off Valentia. Sorting through the refuse, the archeologists found that sea birds were eaten, identifying bones of cormorant, gannet and red-throated diver.

Shellfish was one of the main items of diet. A small quantity of oyster shells and scallop shells was eaten, but most of the time the household dined on limpets and periwinkles, since the midden material contained quantities of their shells. Three pointed pieces of bone found among a huge heap of periwinkles

close to the hearth are assumed to be winkle pickers. A vision is suggested of a family sitting in a dark interior which must have smelt a good deal, close to the fire, listening to the wind and storm raging above them while spearing shellfish and throwing their shells onto the floor.

Small objects discovered included knives and a spoon. A bronze pin, a bone pin and a bone comb all gave clues to age—an eleventh-century date has been suggested, since the comb is similar to the ordinary long comb

used by Vikings. This date and a possible Viking presence is confirmed by the most remarkable find of the excavation.

The main room of the house was approached by a stone-lined passage roofed with lintel stones. The innermost lintel was found to be scratched with lines that formed an inscription. Since part of this inscription was buried in the wall, it was clear that it had been used at an earlier date and when the house was erected it had no significance to the builders.

On the slab, which was of local sandstone, the scratches were found not to be Ogham,

but a Viking inscription in Runic lettering, written in the eleventh-century style. Such lettering, although very different, is organised similarly to Ogham writing. The slab was crumbling and the scratches were indistinct; however, seven words separated by a pocked punctuation were eventually deciphered: LIR . RISTI . STIN . ThINA + [MUNUIKL]. RISTI. [RUN]. –, Lir Erected This Stone + M... Carved the Runes. Lir is a Celtic personal name, but the words themselves are East-Norse, probably Danish. The forms the inscription takes indicate it was carved during the eleventh century.

Professor O'Kelly surmised that although this carved stone was proof that there had been a Viking visitation of Beginish, there was no evidence that this had been in any way violent or the result of pillage and slaughter. On the contrary, the settlement seems to have been peaceful. "It may be that the Viking who carved the letters had already himself become a Christian and had settled down to live with his Irish friends. The Lir who erected the slab was probably an Irishman and... the inscription gives testimony that Gael and Gall could co-operate when the need arose."

The cross carved between the letters suggests strongly that the Viking may have become a Christian. Certainly there were Christians living in the immediate area. A ruined monastery lies near the east shore of Beginish. Another monastic settlement is to be found on Church Island, an islet over two acres (a hectare) in size connected with Beginish by a curving sand bar and accessible

on foot at very low tide. Here the ruins of an oratory with a corbelled roof and finial with zoomorphic decoration had been known for some time.

The intriguing nature of the Runic stone and the imminent threat of erosion lead to renewed interest in the Church Island remains and a subsequent excavation on Church Island took place in 1955 and 1956. Post holes of a wooden building were found, which was later rebuilt as an imposing stone oratory. Around two houses belonging to a community of monks was the usual debris, even though disposal was made easy by the proximity of the sea. The finding of many objects outside the door suggests that the brethren not only did not bother to throw their garbage over the cliff, but lived outside as much as weather permitted. Weather during the tenth and eleventh centuries may well have been warmer than now.

Like the people on Beginish, the monks on Church Island ate large quantities of shellfish. They ate oats and barley, probably in the form of porridge, and used the straw to thatch their

communal houses. They varied their diet with sea birds: gannet, shag, cormorant, white-fronted goose, and duck. Remains were also found of seal meat. But excavation revealed that much of the brethren's needs came from Valentia or from the mainland. The turf for their fires, their oats and barley, and meat from domestic animals must have been carried over to the islet in currachs. Meat from domestic animals—ox, pig, sheep, goat, and horse—must also have been brought from outside since there was no means of supporting animals on the island.

A grave contained the remains of two people, presumably brethren. But excavation of Church Island raised as many questions as it solved. Finds were limited so it was presumed that when the monastic settlement was abandoned—why?—everything of value was taken. Among the items discarded were a small piece of rough material that could have been the edging of a garment and the decayed remains of a bronze-coated iron bell. This object must have had its place in worship, and why it was abandoned is one of the mysteries of Church Island. It may have been forgotten or perhaps it was already in a broken state when it was discarded.

No pottery was found, which is characteristic of early Christian Irish sites. People used wooden vessels or water skins—a fragment of oxhide from the bottom of a nearby well may

have come from a hide water vessel.

The amount of midden material suggests that the community was not here for any length of time. The stone oratory was a large one, replacing a tiny wooden church, and its construction, like those of other dry-stone ecclesiastical buildings in the area, required a certain amount of labour and skill. That Christian communities should come to this remote and lovely spot was unsurprising. Monasteries are abundant in this part of south-west Kerry, and they include the grandeur of the huts on Skellig Michael a few miles out to sea. It is known that there were a number of monastic sites on Valentia, most of which have been overlaid by their subsequent use as graveyards.

The people, lay or holy, who lived on Beginish and Church Island over several centuries in the early Middle Ages are not mentioned in the Annals or the history books. Their existence, including their contact with the Vikings, appears to be peaceful—there is no sign of rape or violence. The excavations give clues to the lifestyle of these fishermen-farmers and monks. Most importantly, details have been deduced from these finds about the hermits and saints elsewhere who chose contemplative existences on islands all around Ireland. In particular we have some ideas about how the monks on Skellig Michael conducted their austere lives.

THE BLASKET ISLANDS

THE BLASKET ISLANDS

PREVIOUS PAGE: West beyond Dunmore Head towards Great Blasket (left) and Inishtooskert, to the right in the distance.

LEFT: Islander Peats Team Ó Cearnigh, photographed on Blasket in about 1940.

ABOVE: An Tiaracht, where the lighthouse and living quarters were built precariously on the side of the massive rock face.

The Blaskets—*na Blascaodaí*—encompass a cluster of six islands and a number of small outlying rocks off the Kerry coast whose jagged and looming shapes can be made out from the old famine road that winds around Slea Head. Nearest the mainland is Beginish, the Little Island, small and flat, whose grass was always considered good for grazing. Beyond, the other islands are arranged in a rough square: Inishtooskert to the north, Inishvickillane and Inishnabro to the south-west. Far to the west is Inishtearaght, whose pinnacles of rock support a lighthouse to which emigrants sailing past to America could wave farewell.

In this world of roaring winds and big seas the Great Blasket, *An Oileán Tiar*, stands out paramount. A drowned mountain range of Old Red Sandstone similar to Slea Head on the facing peninsula, it has been described as "wallowing like a whale in the darkening sea surrounded by her young." It is six-and-a-half kilometres (four miles) long and three-quarters of a kilometre (half a mile) wide, and rises at two points to 300 metres (nearly a thousand feet). Up on a high point was a signal tower until lightning destroyed it in 1934. The land running back to the Black Head, *Ceann Dubh*, is knife-edged and a constant danger; over the years the cliffs falling away to the ocean claimed a number of victims, including sons of the most famous islanders, Tomás Ó Criomhtháinn and Peig Sayers.

Traces of early settlement are scattered on the islands. On the Great Blasket an Iron Age promontory fort can be found on the north-west end located on the edge of a cliff. Another promontory fort is on Inishnabro, so inaccessible that it seems almost perverse that people would build there. Elsewhere monastic cells and clochans indicate that monks of the early Christian era made their usual search for isolation and discomfort. On the great cliffs of Inishtooskert is a small oratory dedicated to St Brendan the Navigator, and three stone crosses and four clochans, or beehive huts, one of which was lived in by a number of families during the nineteenth century. On Inishvickillane, still inhabited as a holiday home by the ex-Taoiseach (Prime Minister), Charles J. Haughey, there are a number of clocháns and another small church dedicated to St Brendan, whose base at Mount Brandon is across the water to the south-east. An Ogham stone bearing the words *Or Do Macrued U Dalach*, Pray for Macruel, Grandson of Dalach, has been removed to Trinity College for safe keeping.

LEFT: Cathedral Rocks, the haunt of seals on Inishnabro, the island of the quernstone.
ABOVE: Inishvickillane has a solitary house – Charles Haughey's holiday home – on its summit.

A census taken in 1835 showed that a few people were making a bare living on Inishtooskert, Beginish, and Inishvickillane. The last still had six inhabitants at the turn of the century until they moved over to the Great Blasket to join the community that inhabited the north-facing, sunless group of little houses known simply as *An Baile* or The Village. This looked out on the looming mainland, the mountains behind Slea Head and the treacherous waters of the sound, which had to be negotiated to reach Dunquin and the attractions of civilisation.

Between the mainland and the Great Blasket stretch the dangerous waters of Blasket Sound where the Armada galleon the *Santa Maria de la Rosa*, armed with 26 guns, struck a reef known as the Stromboli reef after a later shipwreck on September 21, 1588. The force of 297 fighting men included the Prince d'Ascoli, the illegitimate son of the king of Spain. Over the years other wrecks provided a regular bonanza for the inhabitants of the Great Blasket as their flotsam was washed up. In his autobiography Tomás Ó Criomhtháinn described one where "the white strand was covered with beams of red and white deal, white planks, a fragment of a wrecked ship, a chair, a stool, apples and all sorts ….” When the first boxes of tea were washed up on the White Strand some time in the nineteenth century, it was mistaken for dye and used that way until it was correctly identified.

The islanders had to be self-sufficient. Fishing and communication with the mainland depended on their fleet of tarred black currachs known as *naomhóga*. In them the post came over from Dunquin, and often cattle tied with ropes were balanced in these frail craft as they crossed the sound. Slightly smaller boats were used for lobster fishing, which provided a valuable source of outside income—in the 1930s they sold in Dingle for nine shillings a dozen. When the Congested Districts Board made its improvements, including five new houses and a new road, the breakwater pier they provided was inexplicably inadequate. Hardly a year passed without some tragedy on the sea.

On the limited acreage of suitable land the soil, manured with seaweed, produced abundant potatoes to be eaten with buttermilk and fresh milk. Seaweed also was the source of a drink called sleadaí. Domestic and wild fowl, including puffins, sea birds’ eggs, fish, and rabbits provided additional items in the diet. Corn, wheat, and hay for animals were also grown. Donkeys provided transport and the means by which turf was brought from the bog to the houses of An Baile. In addition to cattle, sheep were kept, and the women wove homespun, Although their clothes had none of the beauty of those of the Aran islanders, the women had a simple uniform of a crossover shawl and apron that indicated their married status.

At the beginning of the century close to two hundred people lived on the island, but after the First World War numbers dwindled inexorably. Thereafter there was a series of declines. The fishing the men did could not compete with foreign trawler fleets; the

TOP: *An Baile*, The Village, as it was during the years when it was occupied and, above, as it is now.

An Trá Bhán, the White Strand, can be seen directly beyond it.

remoteness and lack of communication were increasingly wearing. There were no shops or other facilities, and for many years the islanders relied on seal oil for their light. (Seals were also eaten.) They had been cutting away at the turf for hundreds of years, and when that fuel ran out and there was only furze and heather to burn, they had a further impetus for leaving.

The nearest church was at Dunquin. In the school the most essential subject was English, to prepare the children for emigration—many of them would go to Springfield, Massachusetts. On the walls of the school house a picture of an apple tree attracted great interest, since the children had never seen a tree.

The wonder was that a hard and dangerous life on the island lasted for so long. But it left an enduring legacy. The people of An Baile would become famous because their lives were hard and a number of them were geniuses. The tradition of story-telling, poetry, and songs had survived the menace of English and in due course reached a wider public with the aid of outside intervention. From the nineteenth century onward a formidable number of scholars and travellers were attracted to this stronghold where Gaelic culture survived in all its vigour. To their joy they even found men and women who did not know any English at all.

Whether the extraordinary literary ability of a number of islanders would have reached the world without the aid of these visitors is very doubtful. The folklorist whose efforts first focused attention on Blasket was the English scholar and translator of Irish Robin

AFTER a while we heard The Sound,
"ding dong, ding dong", soon after
when The fog cleared, Magread saw
The Lights, and what did we noticed
but a big steamer,

Flower, who spent many summers on the island. Not only did Flower write a sympathetic account of the inhabitants of the Great Blasket, but he translated into English *An t-Oileánach*, the classic autobiography of Tomás Ó Criomhtháinn, as *The Islander*. In his foreword Flower wrote: "The experience of these islanders is necessarily narrow in its range, but within that range is absolute and complete. At sea and on the hill, in the house, in the field, or on the strand, they must at all times be prepared for any event—there is always a narrow margin between them and famine or violent death, and their faculties are the keener for that."

Ó Criomhtháinn, who reared ten children on a smallholding, had been encouraged by a young Gaelic enthusiast, Brian Ó Ceallaigh, to write down his memories of a rich and varied lifestyle that bordered on the medieval. The result, which was first published in Irish in 1929, has been described by the poet Máire Mhac an tSaoi as "one of the solid achievements of Irish literature." But in the prevailing puritanical times, passages were censored and even the most harmless sexual references were ruthlessly expunged.

Peig Sayers, known as "the Queen of the Story-tellers," and born in 1873, spent much of her life on the Great Blasket. Flower wrote of her gift: "her words could be written down as they leave her lips, and they would have the effect of literature with no savour of the artificiality of composition." In due course they were, and today Peig is considered an Irish classic (or the bane of schoolchildren).

Another autobiography by Muiris Ó Súileabháin, *Fiche Bliain ag Fás*, translated by Moya Llewelyn Davies and George Thomson as *Twenty Years a-Growing*, was translated into many languages. But Irish speakers prefer Ó Criomhtháinn's gruff unvarnished Irish, which achieves his aim as he wrote "to set down the character of the people about me so that some record of us might live after us, for

"Great Blasket…wallowing like a whale in the darkening sea surrounded by its twelve young"

SEAN O'FAOLAIN

the like of us will never be seen again." These authors and others who contributed to what has been described as "the Blasket Island library" were all conscious that the things that they had known were vanishing very fast.

Today the Great Blasket is a place of ghosts. Fast boats bring you out on good days to the little pier, which is still inadequate. To the right of the deserted village is *An Trá Bhán*, the White Strand, where seals still congregate and where the islanders played at hurling. Ó Criomhtháinn describes a game played on Christmas Day when men on both sides drove each other in and out of the water.

Above the harbour rise the cottages with their shoulders to the sea stepped up the steep north face. They can still be identified: the house of Eoghan Bán, the weaver, the

house of Séan Cheaist Ó Catháin, the musician, the Board house where Peig Sayers lived. Most are in ruins, although a rough black roof has been fitted over the tiny cottage that was occupied by Ó Criomhtháinn, his wife, and his five sons and two daughters, many of whom died tragically. The *Bóithrín na Marbh*, the Road of the Dead, is still there, down which the deceased were carried to the naomhóg in the harbour waiting to take the coffin over to Dunquin for burial.

By 1940 there were 100 people. After the school shut in 1942, it was only a matter of time before the Great Blasket was returned to nature. Numbers were reduced to 50 by 1947; when the final evacuation took place in 1953 there were only 21 people left to make the last journey over the sound. They began to leave

on Tuesday, November 17, 1953. It was late in the year and they could not face another winter. They went over in two groups—on separate days because the weather was so bad—to Dunquin and their new houses beside a church, a pub, a priest, and a doctor. The houses looked across the sound to their old home.

When I last visited the Great Blasket in a late September I had the feeling that human contradictory voices had only just been stilled. There were the rabbits, and gulls, and terns, and wide perspectives of sky and sea, and there was the view back to the mountainous shoreline of Dunquin, and Slea Head. The lives of the islanders seemed as remote as that of those early monks who built their cells and oratories more than a thousand years ago.

SCATTERY

SCATTERY

Scattery is suffused with legend and tall stories involving a saint, a monster, a golden bell which fell from the heavens into west Clare, a miraculous tree, a visit from the archangel Raphael, magic pebbles, pirates, and a wicked landlord, who, like so many others, has assumed the status of ogre.

Scattery is suffused with legend and tall stories involving a saint, a monster, a golden bell which fell from the heavens into west Clare, a miraculous tree, a visit from the archangel Raphael, magic pebbles, pirates, and a wicked landlord, who, like so many others, has assumed the status of ogre.

The name of Scattery Island, *Inis Chathaigh*, may refer to Cata, the monster expelled by St Senán. Or it may derive from the Norse word for treasure, so that here is a real treasure island. The Vikings established a base here for their raiding parties, trading with other Norse settlements further up the Shannon. Some historians consider that this base may well have predated that of Limerick. The strategically placed island at the mouth of the river was a favourite landfall after raids on the continent of Europe, and the Vikings would tack their longships far out into the Atlantic to catch the west winds that would bring them directly here. We can speculate how they buried their booty, of which two fragments survive. Two ninth-century silver brooches now in the British Museum found near "St Senán's Abbey" on Scattery are Viking in origin.

From the town of Kilrush the island, with its round tower pointing to the sky, seems to float; the ancient monastic buildings crouching around it are just visible. During the summer a regular boat service from the marina (opened in 1991) departs several times a day. Scattery is a river island, but the tide flows up to Limerick, the sea is just beyond, so that the surrounding waters are a brackish mixture of salt and fresh.

At the pier a line of cottages and houses suggests life. But as the boat approaches it becomes obvious that Scattery has succumbed completely to the island malaise and is now deserted. Thatched roofs have fallen in, doors and windows gape open, a piece of rusty corrugated iron gleams in the sun. The roofless schoolhouse accommodated over sixty children in the 1930s.

St Senán founded the great monastery which by Elizabethan times had become ruinous. He was born near Kilrush of a well-to-do family. While guarding his father's cattle he heard a wave breaking behind him as he walked near the seashore and was inspired to take up the holy life. He broke his spear, made it into a cross and went off to study for the Church. His principal foundation was at Scattery, where he is assumed to be buried, having died in A.D.544.

Traditionally there were 11 churches here,

PREVIOUS PAGE: The Collegiate Church of Saints Mary and Senán dates back to the seventh century. The round tower is the tallest in Ireland.

LEFT: The lighthouse standing at the southern end of the island, overlooking Scattery Roads, is a guide to ships making their way up the river Shannon.

ABOVE: The round tower rising from the low line of Scattery seen from near Kilrush. Loop Head and the mouth of the Shannon lie beyond.

and what survives of Senán's foundation must be a fraction of what had once been a great collegiate church which in 1359 had its own bishop. The most imposing ruin is the church of St Mary and St Senán, standing behind the village, a much-altered Romanesque building whose south windows were probably replaced in the fifteenth century. Above the Gothic window at the east end is the stone head of a bishop in his mitre, said to be St Senán himself; a double-headed mythical serpent, possibly meant to represent the Cata, the monster who opposed him, hangs beneath.

To the west stands the round tower, which at 36 metres (120 feet) high is the tallest in Ireland. It has survived hurricanes and lightning, and perhaps marauding Vikings. These towers, which have been considered Ireland's only contribution to world architecture, had a dual function as belfry and as watch tower. The height of Scattery's tower meant that a lookout could see far down the estuary to where longships might be rowing up the river

towards the monastery. However, since its entrance is at ground level, it may have been constructed during a period of relative peace. (One other round tower, at Devinish, has a similar entrance.)

Nearby is a deep rectangular well, St Senán's Well, famous for miracles. During a drought the archangel Raphael showed the saint where to find water, using a holly branch as diviner; this was then planted and became a sacred holly tree. A pattern – assembly – used to be held around this well on Easter Monday; when islanders could not get to the mainland for Mass, they would pray here.

Other medieval remains on Scattery include *Teampall Senán,* where Senán is believed to be buried; an early grave slab beside it asks for a prayer for Moinach, tutor of Mogron. On the highest point of the island there is a wide embracing view looking down the Shannon estuary towards the Heads. Here are the scattered remnants of Árd na nAingeal, to which spot Senán was carried by

the archangel Raphael to confront the monster Cata, which he expelled from the island; according to one theory Cata was a collective name for a tribe of wild cats.

Before the small lighthouse on the east of the island was built in 1868, pilots would light fires here as an aid to ships navigating the Shannon waters. Beside the lighthouse stands the battery, one of six built in the area—as usual, to counter any invasion by Napoleon. The D-shaped fortress is surrounded by a dry moat; six guns were arranged around the curved part of the perimeter, with two howitzers mounted on the roof of the blockhouse. There can be no greater contrast to the holy buildings associated with the ascetic saint than this great stone-blocked building.

Beside the landing pier is *Teampall na Marbh,* the Church of the Dead, probably

ABOVE LEFT: For centuries St Senán's Well effected cures and also supplied the islanders with water.
ABOVE RIGHT: A grave slab at Teampall Senán, bearing inscriptions requesting prayers to be said.

dating from the fourteenth century; the forest of gravestones testifies to the number of people who wished to be buried on holy ground. Near the pier is the remains of a castle built by the Ó Cahane clan around 1577. For centuries the Ó Cahane, who held the title of Coarbs of Senán, were the traditional custodians of the golden bell of Senán, the *Clog an Óir* used in swearing rituals; if a witness gave false testimony after he had sworn on it, he was struck dead. Sold in the nineteenth century, the *Clog an Óir* may be the bronze hand bell typical of those used in monasteries which is now in the British Museum in London. Its elaborately decorated shrine is in the National Museum in Dublin.

The Ó Cahane turned Protestant, spelt their name Keane and became associated

RIGHT: The ruined vaults of the castle built by the Ó Cahane clan in around 1577.

BELOW: The rectangular block house, or barrack, built to the rear of the D-shaped battery.

with the landlord class. In the 1840s Marcus Keane was agent for the landlord of the island, his father-in-law, the Marquis of Conyngham. He built a fishing lodge and spent each summer on the island. An amateur historian, he was one of those who evolved the theory that round towers were phallic symbols—perhaps one reason for his reputed unpopularity.

In 1843 pilots from Kilbaha on the mainland salvaged a dismasted ship, the *Windsor Castle*, out from Bombay. By way of compensation, Marcus Keane offered them land on

the island. It was said that this was the first time that freehold land was bought from landlords in this way.

From Scattery the Kilbaha men continued their role as pilots. At the sight of an incoming ship they would race out in their black currachs; the winner would put his mark on the vessel, and would then navigate it up-stream through sandbanks and currents to a safe berth at Limerick.

Those pilots, like other sailors, would have carried stones from the island drilled with holes and worn as necklaces—charms that prevented them from drowning. When they built their currachs these, too, would also have been provided with St Senán's pebbles for their safety and at their launching would have sailed *deiseal*, clockwise or "sunwise" around the island for protection.

From a high point in 1881 of 141 souls the population declined relentlessly. Today, Scattery has long been deserted.

Many a grassy extensive island
In the bright compass of its courses
From Limerick city to Loop Head,
Of the number is the Isle of Inis Cathy
On which a saint of glorious life
Senán, placed eleven churches,
And a beautiful high clogas beside them.

So wrote a Gaelic poet in his praise of the Shannon River. I visited the island in late summer when the old cultivated fields had gone back to weeds—thistles, daisies, and sheets of ragweed, golden as St Senán's holy bell. From Árd na nAingael towards the south west the river widened between the shores of Limerick and Clare at its approach to the sea. Among deserted fields, riddled with rabbit holes and strewn with the ruins of holy places, the particular atmosphere that lingers on so many of Ireland's islands associated with saints seemed to be intensified on this treeless, eerily beautiful slab of land...

BIBLIOGRAPHY

AA Touring Guide to Ireland. Basingstoke, 1976.

Bence Jones, Mark, *Irish Country Houses.* London, 1988.

Broderick, Mary, *History of Cobh.* Cork, 1989.

Chambers, Anne, *Granuaille—The Life and Times of Grace O'Malley.* Dublin, 1979.

Clark, Wallace, *Rathlin.* Coleraine, 1995.

Concannon, Kieran, ed., *Inishbofin.* Athlone, 1997.

Crossley-Holland, Kevin, *Pieces of Land.* London, 1975.

Cullen, Ciara, and Gill, Peter, *Clare Island Series.* Mayo, 1990.

Fox, Robin, *The Tory Islanders.* London, 1978.

Durell, Penelope, *Discover Dursey.* Cork, 1996.

Haratt, George, *Scattery Island.* Clare, 1995.

Harbison, Peter, *Guide to National and Historic Monuments of Ireland.* Dublin, 1975.

Heraughty, Patrick, *Inishmurray.* Dublin, 1996.

Killanin, Lord, and Duignan, Michael V., *The Shell Guide to Ireland.* Dublin, 1962.

Kruger, Chuck, *Cape Clear—Island Magic.* Cork, 1994.

Lavelle, Des, *The Skellig Story.* Dublin, 1992.

Lehane, Brendan, *Wild Ireland.* London, 1995.

McCormick, Donald, *Islands of Ireland.* Reading, 1974.

Mac Conghail, Muiris, *The Blaskets—People and Literature.* Dublin, 1988.

McDonald, Theresa, *Achill Island.* Tullamore, 1997.

McGowan, Jo, *Inishmurray.* Sligo, 1998.

McNally, Kenneth, *The Islands of Ireland.* London, 1975.

Malins, Edward, and Bowe, Patrick, *Irish Gardens and Demesnes from 1830.* London, 1980.

Mason, Thomas H., *The Islands of Ireland.* Dublin, 1936.

Maxwell, W. H., *Wild Sports of the West.* London, 1832.

Murray's Handbook for Travellers in Ireland, 1878.

Neeson, Eoin, *The Book of Irish Saints.* Cork, 1967.

Newby, Eric, and Petry, Diana, *Wonders of Ireland.* London, 1969.

O'Cleirigh, Nellie, *Valentia. A Different Irish Ireland.* Dublin, 1992.

O'Kelly, Michael J., *An Island Settlement at Beginish, Co Kerry.* Proceedings of the Royal Irish Academy, 1958.

O'Kelly, Michael J., *Church Island Near Valencia, Co. Kerry.* Proceedings of the Royal Irish Academy, 1960.

O'Brien, Daniel M., *Beara—A Journey Through History.* Cork, 1991.

O'Reilly, Dolly, *Sherkin Island.* Cork, 1990.

Payne-Gallwey, *The Fowler In Ireland.* Southampton, 1885.

Praeger, Robert Lloyd, *The Way that I Went.* Dublin, 1936.

Robinson, Tim, *Stones of Aran—Pilgrimage.* Dublin, 1986.

Roche, Richard, and Merne, Oscar, *Saltees—Islands of birds and legends.* Dublin, 1977.

Somerville-Large, Peter, *Cappaghglass.* London, 1985.

Somerville-Large, Peter, *The Coast of West Cork.* London, 1972.

Somerville-Large, Peter, *The Grand Irish Tour.* London, 1981.

Synge, J. M., *The Aran Islands.* London, 1907.

INDEX

ACKNOWLEDGEMENTS AND CREDITS

Author's acknowledgements
I would like to thank Ciara Cullen for finding me copies of the excellent Clare Island Series which she co-authored with Peter Gill. Also Gillian, my wife, for all her help, in spite of being seasick.

Photographer's acknowledgements
I would personally like to thank the many people who made this book such a pleasure to photograph. If the Irish people are known as a hospitable race, then the islands may well be where they were schooled in their ways. My thanks for their help and patience to the staff of Cobh Museum, The Skellig Experience, Inishbofin Heritage Centre, Rathlin Island Museum, Valentia Heritage Centre, The Blasket Centre, and the Office of Public Works. My gratitude to Owen Walsh and Patrick Corcoran for bouncing me across the waves of Skellig and Valentia; to David McCollum and Liam McFaul for their company on Rathlin and to Brian Hughes for his hospitality in Clifden; to Maria O'Connell for again trying to keep me organised, to Duncan Harrison who processes all my films (and so sees all my mistakes), and to Chris Ireland who helps to keep me and my cameras on the road. My especial thanks to Mick Hennessy of Irish Helicopters, both for his companionship and his immaculate skills as a pilot. It was a joy to fly with you over these dramatic waters. To many people I owe a few pints, and I hope to enjoy your company again in these special island homes.

*

All photographs in this book were specially taken by David Lyons, except those supplied by the organisations on the following pages—Blasket Heritage Centre: 128, 131 (above right), 132 (above); Graceanne Duffy: 55 (above left); Quadrillion Publishing Ltd: 9, 11, 19 (above right); Rathlin Island Museum: 57–8, 61 (above right); Slidefile: 62–7; Valentia Heritage Centre: 117.

Many thanks to the following for their help: Fleur Robertson (copy editing); Kathie Gill (proof reading and indexing); Maggi McCormick (Americanising); Mark Buckingham (mapmaking).

Credits

Designer
Justina Leitão

Project Editor
Simon Tuite

Publishing Director
Will Steeds

Art Director
Philip Chidlow

Production
Neil Randles